S0-BOC-094

GETTING NOWHERE

BY THE SAME AUTHOR

THE LANGUAGE OF GRACE

BT
738
.H33
1985

getting nowhere

christian hope & utopian dream

peter s. hawkins

GOSHEN COLLEGE LIBRARY
GOSHEN, INDIANA

© 1985 by Cowley Publications. All rights reserved.

Printed in the United States of America.

Library of Congress Cataloging in Publication Data

Hawkins, Peter S., 1945-
   Getting nowhere.

   Bibliography: p.
   1. Sociology, Christian. 2. Hope. 3. Utopias. I. Title
BT738.H33 1985   260   85-12758
ISBN 0-936384-28-X

COWLEY PUBLICATIONS
980 MEMORIAL DRIVE
CAMBRIDGE, MA 02138

H-13-88

B18/MJ

To John Cook and David Kelsey,
colleagues for a decade
and fellow-travelers to utopia.

PREFACE

With the approach of 1984 many a teacher's thoughts turned not only to George Orwell's ominous novel, but to the more ancient dream that lay behind its nightmare—utopia. We at the Yale Divinity School were no exception, and so together with my colleagues John Cook and David Kelsey I participated in a course that set out to explore the theological dimensions of a topic most often treated as an entirely secular phenomenon. For all three of us it was a brave new world of academic pursuit, to which we brought both our several disciplines and our pleasure in working together. My thinking about ideal community was fostered entirely in their company, and out of a year's planning and teaching with them the substance of this book developed. In acknowledgement of this debt, therefore, I dedicate my work to them, to friends who not only helped me to understand the significance of utopia as a topic for study, but who also gave me a measure of its experience. For surely in the best of all possible worlds one would work and learn and laugh as I did with colleagues like these.

During the summer of 1984, the Chautauqua Institution gave me the opportunity to refine the work I had prepared for class and to present it more formally before a larger audience. I am thankful to Dr. William Jackson for inviting me to deliver the series of lectures which later became the first draft of this book. Every afternoon for a week I was encouraged by a lively audience of inveterate Chautauquans, convinced they knew the specifications of utopia first-hand. It was often easy to believe them, at least when in the care of Gwen Read, Winny Llewelyn, Barry Vaughan and Carey Anne Meyer.

The manuscript of *Getting Nowhere* was produced in two stages. Under the guidance of Dr. Luis Varela I learned to write with the assistance of a word processor; he also restrained the Luddite in me and on a number of occasions kept the hardware from being hurled out the window. It was then that Cynthia Shattuck came to the rescue, helping me to see that with the freedom to write on a computer also came the tendency to write too much. It was a painful lesson, but one for which I (and certainly all of my readers) stand in gratitude. No doubt there are some who would eliminate editors from citizenship in utopia, even as Thomas More banished lawyers and Plato banned the poets. But I know an ideal when I see one and count myself blessed to have Cynthia Shattuck's unerring blue pencil even as I have the constancy of her friendship.

Peter Hawkins

CONTENTS

getting nowhere

At the beginning of the 1970's, when for better or for worse many Americans felt as if they stood on the brink of a new world, I found myself at a conference center tucked away in a particularly beautiful corner of the New England countryside. I was there, together with a friend from graduate school, to attend a meeting of academic luminaries whose blessed company we had each recently been asked to join. We approached the three days of meeting with great expectations, assuming that there—in the society of humanists renowned for intellect and sensibility, and with all our physical needs amply taken care of— we would experience some better "way" than we had found in the mundane circles of our own university, let alone in the violent world outside the campus. Although our retreat would last for a mere three days, we came looking for the "good place" of our longings, for that ideal arrangement of enlightened minds that kept us hopeful in the midst of Kent State and Viet Nam. Ours was a more conventional and bookish version of the same dream that sent other of our contemporaries on the road to Esalen and Woodstock and a thousand upstate communes; we all hoped by one means or another to get ourselves back into the Garden. There had to be a better way to live, and for us the route seemed to lead straight into the groves of academe.

Every attempt to return to Eden, however, suffers its own reenactment of the Fall. By the end of the second day, we realized to our dismay the extent to which these high-powered professors of the humanities had, step by step, undermined everything we thought the humanities to stand for. Arrogant, posturing, vain, fiercely competitive: they turned every question and answer period into an ordeal of wits, every conversation over coffee into a contest of supremacy. The game was a sophisticated version of King of the Mountain, and as we watched in dismay whole rooms full of contestants attempted to scale the slippery

slopes, stepping on those they fancied below them, even as they
worked doggedly to dethrone the person standing (however
momentarily) at the top. I thought about joining the Peace Corps.

On the morning of the third day, our hearts sinking with each
new record in one-upmanship, my friend mentioned (in a desperate attempt at comic relief) an aboriginal group living in New
Zealand which she had recently read about in a book by Claude
Lévi-Strauss. They had been "civilized" in the last century by
British settlers who taught them, among far more dubious lessons,
the game of rugby. In learning the sport, however, this indigenous
population made it truly their own, adapting its alien assumptions
to fit the rules by which they were accustomed to live. And so,
to the astonishment of visiting anthropologists (and the disgruntled
graduate students who read their findings), these extraordinary
New Zealanders would play rugby day in and day out, sometimes
for as long as a week at a time, determined to keep the game going
for as long as it would take until the decisive moment had
arrived—the moment when both sides had finally reached a tie
score. Then, and only then, might the game end.

My response to this refreshing news from across the sea, which
seemed to blow through that conference center like a fresh ocean
breeze, was to wish there and then that we could all "go native."
How wonderful it would be if everyone might play the academic
or professional game according to *their* rules—not to win at all
costs, but rather for the sheer mutual pleasure of the experience
of playing! What began as a self-defense against depression and
boredom, moreover, became a more serious, more sustained con-
jecture as the last day of the meetings wore on. I began to see
the conference in a different light, as if it all might be otherwise.

What I began to imagine was a restructuring of this microcosm
of academia, one that would return these savage professors to the
principles of civilization expressed in the spirit of this amiable
New Zealand rugby game. What if, for instance, every paper read
at the conference had stressed its debt to other thinkers, rather
than protesting its originality? What if people working in the
humanities were organized on the model of a team, with an
emphasis on communal research and support rather than on the
isolated (and supposedly independent) individual contribution?
What if all academic work were published anonymously? What
then would it be like to sit next to Professor X at lunch, or listen

to a panel of experts discuss "the current state of literary study"?
O brave new world!

What I am describing here, in my reconstruction of a daydream that saved the day over a decade ago, is a rudimentary act
of imaginative reform—a miniature and quite spontaneous version
of the more deliberate dreaming I want to explore in subsequent
chapters. It began, you recall, with shattered expectations and the
sense of alienation that followed in their wake. This seems to be
the precondition of every vision of social change: a sense that
reality has disappointed our hopes and left us with less than our
fair share of life's blessing. In my own case, while I had expected
this gathering of the brightest and the best to be a little bit of
heaven on earth, what I found on the contrary was a travesty of
human association—a dynamic doomed to bring out the very worst
in people and frustrate the possibility of genuine community.
I had the presence of mind and strength of conviction to know
I wanted "out."

One way to have acted on this rejection might have been to
flee the scene entirely, rushing headlong into the solitude of the
Berkshire hills or the distractions of the nearby mall. I could have
been content to cultivate my personal garden and otherwise (as
they used to say) "drop out." Instead, however, I unconsciously
resorted to the time-honored survival technique of thinkers from
Plato to our own time. I imagined the healthy obverse of what I
saw before me: the paradigm of community locked within this
parody. And with the sea change offered me in the example of
those native New Zealanders at play, I began mentally to rearrange
custom and hierarchy and value so as to create an environment
that might foster our humanity rather than inhibit its growth and
flourishing. The result would be rich and strange indeed.

Of course at the time my thoughts were only beginning to
take shape. I had not yet pushed myself to consider the consequences of my renovation of the academic life, or the theory of a
fulfilled human nature that undergirded it, or even broached the
crucial issue of what it would take to inaugurate (let alone
enforce) my new regime. Nor had I assessed what it would mean
to me personally to lose the possibility of claiming an "individual"
discovery in scholarship, or never to see my own name on a book I
had written. There were other questions as well. What would be
the effect of an argument never being won? Would team spirit

preclude the show of brillance, the dazzle of an individual mind idiosyncratically at work? Would Professor X in the end be a better partner over lunch, or in my new academy would I merely have gotten his blandness in exchange for the more colorful display of his arrogance? I had not yet tried to live in my own paradise. Nonetheless, I had assembled the raw materials of reform and found in them no small measure of self-defense. I turned my nay-saying into something positive, and if only in the territory of my mind, I laid the groundwork for change. After all, what if our life together *could* be different? What if we changed this or that premise, altered our priorities, engineered our environment along rational lines instead of simply accepting as an unchangeable given the folly we have inherited? What might the world look like then?

Furthermore, in turning my disgust over the behavior of those distinguished professors into a vision of how they might come to interact more humanely, I was inadvertently following the double movement that all imaginative social reform seems to entail. Beginning with a "No" hurled in the face of the status quo, I worked through that simple negation toward a tentative and exploratory "Yes." It was not satisfying enough simply to reject and withdraw. Some spirit of optimism, some deep-seated and unexamined desire to meddle and improve, led me for a few moments to reimagine reality. And so, if only within the empire of fantasy, I tried on a new world for size. I could speculate on the condition of true human fulfillment and then, in my mind's eye, watch its golden towers rise up out of the rubble around me.

In this act of revision there was no place for half-measures or patchwork amelioration. I wanted my professors not simply to wear feathers and paint and affect a temporary change of heart; I wanted them to *be* different. My mind longed for radical reform—the complete conversion of warring academics into peaceful aborigines, playing the old academic game in a wholly new way. Using the materials at hand, I envisioned a new creation. Thus, underneath the sheer fun of turning the accustomed world upside down, I was in fact entertaining some of the most basic questions that anyone can pose. Who are we? What kind of society would most deeply fulfill our nature? What would it take for us to be "at home" with one another? What would the world be like if we had presided over it "in the beginning," mapping out

the contours of a creation a little less fallen than our own? I
began, in other works, to imagine utopia.

* * *

Our exploration of the phenomenon has to begin with the
word itself. When Thomas More was in search of a name to give
his fantasy island—a name that would convey the seriousness with
which he took his book-long joke—he coined a word that with-
drew with one hand the credibility it extended with the other. He
achieved this verbal sleight-of-hand by taking the Greek noun for
"place," *topos*, and prefixing it with a mysteriously ambivalent
"u." His learned audience was quick to enjoy the confusion,
because More's prefix could be played out in either of two directions. It could be taken as the Greek "eu," meaning good, ideal,
perfect, or, on the other hand, taken as "ou," indicating an
absence or deficiency. A linguistic hermaphrodite from birth,
"utopia" might point either to the happy place of one's dreams
("eu-topia") or to no place at all ("ou-topia"). Better yet, it
might suggest both realities at once, so that for the person able to
keep opposite notions in mind simultaneously, to speak of utopia
would be at once to affirm "a place, state, or condition ideally
perfect in respect to politics, laws, customs, and conditions" (to
quote the Oxford English Dictionary) and, at the same time, to
deny the existence of any such thing.

From the very beginning English usage has confirmed the
ambivalence that More intended in his etymological play, for with
the first appearance of the word in 1516 utopia has been used to
praise *and* to dismiss, to indicate a dream come true *and* to dispel
a chimerical fantasy. But unfortunately, while More intended his
pun to convey senses and nonsense at once, utopia has largely
inspired an attitude of either/or: either we have a belief in the
possibility of ideal human flourishing within a perfect community
(and use the word *in bono*) or we hold to a scepticism that
would say with Macauley, "An acre in Middlesex is better than a
principality in utopia." Anywhere, in other words, is better than
nowhere.

The reader might assume that any book which called itself
Getting Nowhere would clearly have made up its mind on the
subject and enrolled in the ranks of the nay-sayers. The title,

after all, recalls a familiar expression of futility and despair. It is a phrase people use when they find themselves running in circles or pushing up against locked doors—when they find themselves "getting nowhere." Presumably the author of such a book would consider anyone who nurtured utopian hopes to be a kind of Sisyphus figure, toiling up the unscalable slopes but doomed to be crushed by the sheer weight of frustration and failure on the painful way down.

This is not at all what I intend. Rather, I want to signal through my title a desire to play along with Thomas More in his game of ambivalence—his now-you-see-it-now-you-don't. I want to explore what value a fantasy of communal perfection might have when brought to bear on the imperfect communities in which we live, to assess the benefits of attending to "nowhere." For like Thomas More, I see real merit in a journey that has no concrete destination, but whose primary rewards are to be discovered in the journeying itself. Indeed, it seems to me that the major gift of utopian imagining is the process of reflection, clarification, and choice it entails; in the options for change it suggests once we begin to look critically at our social order with a more or less radical eye to revision. As we often experience in actual travel, the preparation and the going itself may very well beat getting there. This, at least, is my own prejudice, stated here at the outset. The best of all possible worlds is precisely the one we long and look for, but which we neither reach, nor build, nor ever have to live in. Utopia is to be fantasized; it is not to be entered into.

I am not concerned here with the admittedly fascinating history of actual utopian experiments, with its record of people putting their notions of ideal community to the test. Instead, I will explore the history of an idea as it has been constructed in literature, in fictions of utopia that in different ways engage More's paradox of fantasy and reality, the "good place" and "no place."[1] Some of the books I consider view themselves as metaphors of ideal community rather than as straightforward representations. They present a utopian solution which in the end cannot be taken as literally perfect, but which, through the fictional experience it offers, leaves the reader restless and questioning, provoked to thought—and perhaps to action. More typical of this literature since the Enlightenment, however, is another strategy altogether. It views utopia as a live option, not as a metaphor of the happy life, but as a blueprint for it. Dissatisfied merely to suggest plausibility, it wants to leap off the page and become reality, inspiring the reader to build its proposed version of Jerusalem in whatever land will bear the construction.

The difference between these two kinds of utopian imagining is profound, both in terms of what they demand and what they deliver. But whether as metaphor or model, whether as a fiction to be interpreted or as a program to be translated more or less directly into action, the works under discussion all open their worlds to the reader who is foolish enough to consider (*pace* Macauley) what it might be like if an acre in Middlesex was indeed annexed by a still more excellent way. Despite substantial disagreement on the uses of utopia (let alone of its meaning), they all demonstrate its power to take us beyond where we stand now. Pushing back against the boundaries of necessity, these schemes of communal fulfillment renew our minds with an enlarged sense of human possibility—and of the surprisingly difficult task of pleasing ourselves.

To speak of the renewing of mind is to recall the Letter to the Romans (12:2): "Do not be conformed to this world, but be transformed by the renewal of your mind." St. Paul, of course, was not enjoining any specific agenda for social reform, or asking his readers to think imaginatively about how Rome itself might be overhauled and renewed in its political structures, its economic base, and its social customs. Paul was not in any meaningful sense of the term a utopian thinker. But if utopia requires a scriptural proof-text, surely it would be found in this verse with its call to be transformed by a new reality, with its extended hope for becoming something utterly new—a hope which the verse goes on to proclaim "good and acceptable and perfect."

In the chapter which is immediately to follow I will suggest how utopian thought has been nourished by biblical notions of a renewed mind and a divine kingdom. From the outset I want to claim that no matter how secular its orientation, utopian imagining is an essentially religious activity. This is not to say that a theological perspective is the last word on the subject, or that it should overshadow the social, economic and ideological factors that have undeniably influenced (and even determined) the course of utopian thought from Thomas More's day until our own. What I want to emphasize here, however, is the penchant of all acts of

utopian imagination to raise up, and to worry over, questions of
ultimate existential concern—religious questions. For in reshaping
our existing world along more ideal lines, we must inevitably come
to some fundamental decisions about who we are, what most
truly fulfills us, and what best enables us to cohere and flourish
communally. Our search to transcend the society we already
know is informed by an idea of transcendence; that is, of some
notion of a truer way to be human. Therefore, while it matters
profoundly to the ultimate shape of a utopia whether or not it is
"open" to the divine, we can still speak about it as a religious
phenomenon even if God, like the poets in Plato's *Republic*, has
been banished. For every attempt to imagine the world anew is an
effort to satisfy the most genuine needs and desires of human
identity, to "shape our end" in a way that makes us happy. It
should come as no surprise that the stakes are highest and the
exertion most desperate when the utopian strategist feels called
upon to play God for the benefit of others, either to make up for
a divine absence or to create a world which is "good and acceptable and perfect" beyond God's wildest dreams. The atheist
utopian knows both the exhilaration and the burden of the
creator.

An example of purely theological thinking on this subject is
Paul Tillich's brief but highly suggestive essay, "Critique and
Justification of Utopia."[2] It not only takes seriously the religious
dimension of what is most often treated as a merely secular enterprise, but focuses on another aspect of ambivalence than we have
considered thus far: the simultaneous truth and untruth of utopia.
For Tillich its truth lies in utopia's rootedness in human nature, in
our discontent with the injustice of the world as it is and in our
hopes for a fuller life. Because by nature we are creatures who
hope, in other words, it is necessary for us to have an ideal to
reach for. It provides us with a *telos* for our existence, a goal of
corporate fulfillment that joins private fantasy to the more generous dream of a common life together. More than just a dream, it
is at its best an empowering vision—a vision which urges us first to
"negate the negative in human existence" and then to press
toward some positive goal. Utopia tells the truth about human
being in its liberation of our God-given potential to reshape and
reimagine whatever situation we are given. It is an aspect of our
human creativity, an exercise of the *imago Dei* within us.

Where it tells a lie—or, to vary our discourse, where it commits a heresy—is in its reluctance to admit a limit to our powers and thereby to acknowledge the fallibility and incompletion of human being. Tillich refrains from using traditional Christian language in his essay, but it is clear that what he intends by the "untruth" of utopia is nothing less than the arrogance of the original sin: the desire to be "as gods," enclosed in a world of our own making. In its act of human self-definition, utopia sins by being oblivious; "it forgets the finitude and estrangement of man, it forgets that man as finite is a union of being and non-being, and it forgets that man under the conditions of existence is always estranged from his true or essential being and that it is therefore impossible to regard his essential being as attainable." Utopia forgets, in other words, that we do not have it of ourselves to help ourselves; it ignores our need for grace. It also mistakes what can only be a finite human work for reality itself, thereby losing the dialectical tension which should obtain between possible and impossible, between what we can actually achieve and what we must continue to strive after. Tillich finds the indeterminacy of "nowhere" to be our growing edge, a sign of our openness to what transcends us. The heresy of utopia, on the other hand, is that it forestalls the human journey toward genuine fulfillment by reaching premature conclusions. It can make an idol of its own ideals, imprisoning us in the very structure that was meant to set us free.

One danger of this falsehood is that it will lead to "metaphysical disillusionment" once the false god of human perfection is exposed as impotent. Worse yet, it may inaugurate a reign of terror for the purpose of maintaining order in the twilight of utopian failure. Tillich writes in a century which has seen the realities of both disillusionment and terror. But if these consequences of utopian hope are meant to be avoided, we must keep alive the ideal of a fuller human existence itself, for the sheer fact that such hoping is an integral aspect of ourselves as persons. We live in hope—and not simply of the life to come. Indeed, a sense of responsibility for envisioning a more just human community might well be a part of the church's mission. And yet, at least from Tillich's perspective, the response of traditional Christianity has been to decline the opportunity of utopian renewal. Instead the church has too often retreated into reactionary conservativism, uncritically supporting the authority in power—or has forsaken the world altogether in flights of mysticism and private spirituality. As a result, the political arena has been abandoned to the powers that be or left vulnerable to demonic possiblities.

What Tillich finally calls for is a concept of utopia which, while asking us to strive ceaselessly to "negate the negative in human existence," remains skeptical about all our solutions and provisional about every proposed social "end." He calls for a vision of fulfilled humanity that avoids falling into idolatry by remembering the fallibility of any human construct; by remaining tentative, able to be surprised by new (even contradictory) insight; in short, by being open to the mysterious "last word" which is properly reserved for God's kingdom alone. What keeps utopia honest and benign is its awareness of a transcendent dimension to existence which humanity can never control or fully realize on earth. At its best, it remembers that there is a limit, as well as an extent, to our powers. By negating its own falsehood, and in refusing to worship an idol of its own making, utopia offers an essential expression of the human spirit. It moves us in hope toward the justice of God's kingdom, acknowledging that ultimate destination to be beyond human imagining. For Tillich, then, utopia must be a journeying toward, and never a settling in. It is his twentieth-century version of Augustine's *civitas peregrina*: a process rather than a permanent home.

What I find helpful in Tillich's "Critique and Justification of Utopia" is a theological analysis that enjoys its dreams of fulfillment with eyes wide open, ready for the forces of fantasy and tyranny that stand to corrupt a true act of hope. He sees at once the virtue of deploying the laborers in the vineyard, as well as (to shift Testaments) their susceptibility to raising up golden calves. Or, to express his ambivalence in metaphor that comes still closer to home, he recognizes the necessity of imagining "Jerusalem," but warns all residents of a green and pleasant land to be on their guard. The actual building is dangerous, he seems to say, but the planning of it absolutely essential.

What Tillich does not offer, however, is any consideration of a case in point. His study is entirely generic; he thinks theologically about ideal worlds he never visits. So Tillich does not actually get "nowhere." Nor does the academic tone of his essay suggest the truth of his cardinal point—the rootedness of utopia in our nature. Neither the prerogative of theologians nor political thinkers, novelists nor professional prophets, utopia is, on the contrary, an aspect of the human mind in constant longing for its own renewal. And so, while indebted to Tillich for his analysis, it is the *ordinariness* of this kind of imagining that I want to emphasize here. Despite the library shelves filled with histories, commentaries and books like *Getting Nowhere*, utopia is not only a subject for analysis, but the substance of our dreams. A disillusioned graduate student imagines the perfect academy; friends plan in retirement to take over an island in Maine; politicians fill our heads with visions of "America." In every case, an ideal begins to form—and we start to get nowhere.

The writers I want to explore in this book have all succeeded in carrying to fruition these inchoate acts of utopian imagination. Beyond this shared achievement, however, their constructs are as diverse as the possibilities of utopia itself. For in the house of ideal community there are many mansions indeed. Some glow with hope for what the real world might eventually become; some are terrifying in their exploration of the dream come true. Still others use irony and ambiguity in their presentations of perfection, demanding that readers discern for themselves the true utopia from the false, the genuine act of hope from an exercise in dangerous self-delusion.

The range of religious presupposition among the writers to be considered is also wide. In Thomas More, the founding father of the literary utopia and its most enigmatic exemplar, the whole enterprise gets off to a very Christian start. And yet if one comes to his *De optimo reipublicae* expecting the work of a Catholic apologist and martyr-saint—expecting, that is, to be given one man's vision of an earthly City of God—serious disappointment is in store. To be sure, the commonwealth he describes has realized a measure of justice and equality that puts the Europe of More's day (or the America of our own) to shame. But how far we are to take Utopia's principles as exemplary, let alone believable, is something impossible to determine. The author plays his cards extremely close to his chest by setting his island "nowhere" beyond the borders of Christendom, extolling its praises through a not altogether reliable witness, raising up a supposed mirror of perfection in which there are a sufficient number of flaws to keep us looking elsewhere for the *civitas Dei*. But perhaps it is precisely in Utopia's inadequacy, in the obvious imperfections of so

undeniably happy a place, that More's alternate world approaches
Tillich's category of utopian truth. For what his seminal work
presents us with is a model of social organization which aims at
the greater fulfillment of human needs, but which does not in
itself claim ultimacy. More's ideal human commonwealth remains
open to that greater kingdom still to come. It presents at best a
provisional fulfillment.

There is no such reticence in Edward Bellamy. In moving
from More to Bellamy's *Looking Backward* we travel from the
early sixteenth century to the late nineteenth, from the Ur-text of
this literature to its leading American exemplar, and from utopia as
a metaphor to utopia as a model of perfection meant to be built.
Not content to bring his readers only as far as "nowhere," Bellamy
intends to move them into the Golden Age—into Boston as it
might be in the year 2000—when the gross inequities of the
present time will be transformed by spiritual renewal, advanced
technology, and enlightened national socialism. His utopia is a
portrait of the millenium, but a millenium that has arrived without
Christ. It is a transposition of the heavenly kingdom to our own
cities, neither impeded by human sin nor inaugurated by divine
initiative. Bellamy's work is full of religious fervor, but a fervor
so in love with humanity that it effectively excludes God and any
notion of divine grace. Boston in the year 2000 is still "on the
way," but there is nothing between it and full perfection but sustained human effort. For Bellamy, we have it of ourselves to help
ourselves.

Le Corbusier's *Radiant City*, a manifesto of urban renewal
from the early 1930's, radiates the same confidence and exhilaration that pulses through *Looking Backward*. He too sees the
kingdom at hand, and in ringing prose declares that it is entirely
possible to have utopia now. All that is needed is the courage
and determination to act on the architect's plan; to clear out the
old city and raise up the new; to fulfill our human needs by giving
us the proper environment—light, air, modernity. Le Corbusier's
vision is also millenarian, but its socialist "kingdom" has completely cut loose of any notion of the transcendent. There are no
internal obstacles, nothing between us and our fulfillment but a
failure of vision. Otherwise, as is the case with Bellamy's twenty-
first-century Boston, the Radiant City is ready to bring heaven

down to earth. The dream of an ideal social order awaits only our permission to proceed.

At about the same time that Le Corbusier proclaimed his Radiant City, however, a fear of utopia's "success" provoked a backlash of the imagination. The result was some memorable works of antiutopian fiction, the most famous of which is George Orwell's *1984*. In contrast to the optimism of earlier thinkers, confident in the power of human beings to master their environment and therefore their fate, we have in Orwell a suspicion of mastery of any kind. In the course of a novel which systematically shatters every expectation of hope, he shows the wages of utopian thought to be a bitterly ironic reversal (or grotesque fulfillment) of all its lofty premises. An unbounded faith in human potential can lead to absolute tyranny, while the demand for control and order, rather than enhancing our lives, can lead us close to extinction. And so, with fearful symmetry, utopia's attempt to bring heaven down to earth has given us, in the pages of Orwell's oracular fiction, nothing less than a simulacrum of hell—perhaps the most vivid portrait of damnation that we have in twentieth century literature.

If, as Tillich maintains, the great untruth of utopia is its dismissal of God, the final step in its refusal to acknowledge anything "more" than human supremacy, then Orwell shows with a vengeance the consequences of that denial. This is not to claim the novelist a Christian, but merely to emphasize the central warning of Orwell's cautionary tale: when human beings arrogate the position of divinity for themselves, they become not God, but Satan. The rejection of any notion of a need for grace can unleash a vast and gratuitous evil. What *1984* demonstrates so frighteningly is that absolute confidence in human powers corrupts absolutely, with the result that the act of utopian hope becomes an experience of total despair.

The year before Orwell published his dark forebodings, B.F. Skinner produced the buoyantly utopian *Walden Two* (1948). with its celebration of those same powers of human self-determination that *1984* drew to their logical conclusions. Skinner writes in the line of Bellamy and Le Corbusier, self-assured that something very much like the millennium is within our reach. Thanks to the technology of behavioral engineering, we have

the ability to make people what we want them to be—to make
them happy.

Against this utopian proclamation Walker Percy aims his
wildly satiric *Love in the Ruins* (1971). Every contemporary
solution to human malaise (scientific or humanistic) is mocked,
each scheme to make us healthy exposed as a false cure. Percy
wages his warfare through a protagonist-narrator "Thomas More"
who, as a collateral descendent of the author of *Utopia*, links
this critique of utopian imagination to the man who first started
us getting nowhere. In his "Doctor" More, the novelist gives us a
physician who cannot heal himself, a would-be world savior who
thinks he can weld the broken self whole again. The novel goes on
to dash these aspirations, even as it repudiates every attempt to
control humanity for its own good.

But Percy avoids Orwell's severe pessimism by concluding his
novel on a note of hope. It does not lie in any scheme for social
reform or program of education. Instead, Percy proclaims that it
is possible to live happily in a resolutely imperfect world, not only
by coming to appreciate the beauty of ordinary life even in the
"ruins" of western civilization, but by looking forward to the
coming of a kingdom that escapes all human formulation, that will
never fully be realized here—or be lost in the multiple disasters of
the twentieth century. Unlike the work of the real Thomas More,
which for all its subtle undercutting of perfection nonetheless
risked a tentative image of it, Percy's fiction places all its hopes on
the individual's renewal of mind, in private joys and simple pleasures. It rejects the falsehood of utopia, but at the cost of its
promise—a vision of how *society* might be otherwise. Sharing
More's Christian orthodoxy, but not his interest in how an entire
community might be more fully human, Percy leaves us looking
beyond. Whether this rejection of "nowhere" is a gain or loss, an
assertion of Christian hope or a failure to realize its implications in
the world, is the question to which we will come in the end.

o zion, haste!

I suggested in my opening chapter that the impulse to construct a utopia, whether in fantasy or in fact, begins with a sense of expectations unmet. Because the present has failed to give us either what we want or what we feel we deserve, we change things as they are to create an order of life more suited to ourselves. Discontent with the way things now are irritates the imagination into action, until, like the grain of sand lodged in the shell of an oyster, our disappointment undergoes a sea change into something rich and strange—the world as it should be. The result is a pearl of great price: a social order created with the express purpose of meeting human needs, of making us happy again.

Happy *again*. This sense of a recovery or return is perhaps the most profound sentiment within utopian imagining, for underneath its discontent with the present and its hopes for the future there always stands some longing for the way it used to be—"years ago," in one's childhood, when life was simpler and people were better, in the good old days. Although utopia's reinvention of reality often seems to cast us forward in time, or to land us in another world which is in some sense more forward-looking than our own, its drive invariably takes the form of nostalgia. It draws us backward in time to the "beginning," before what Tillich calls the "negative in human existence" came to dominate our affairs. This may be an earlier period in history, before present corruption closed in around us; but more likely still, it is some fantasy—or, could it be, some recollection?—of a time before time, *in illo tempore*. Utopia always seems to remember, however dimly, a paradise lost.

And for this reason, it is customary to link utopian imagining with that complex of myths which has kept even the darkest stretches of Western culture glimmering with the shared memory of a Golden Age. The *locus classicus* is Hesiod's *Works and Days*, dating from the eighth century B.C.E., which looks backward from

the poet's present through a succession of degenerating epochs to
the happy reign of Kronos that stood pristine and healthy at the
start. It was then that the "golden generation of mortals"

> lived as if they were gods,
>   their hearts free from all sorrow,
> by themselves, and without hard work or pain;
>   no miserable
> old age came their way; their hands, their feet,
>   did not alter.
> They took their pleasure in festivals,
>   and lived without troubles.
> When they died, it was as if they fell asleep.
>   All goods
> were theirs. The fruitful grainland
>   yielded its harvest to them
> of its own accord.[3]

This ancient account of the beginning of human time was
passed on to Roman culture through the religious festival of the
Saturnalia, where for a few days each year common people might
enact their fantasy of life in King Kronos' day, when all were
equal and material possessions held in common.[4] In turn, this
ancient Greek vision was passed on by Rome to Christian Europe
through Ovid's *Metamorphoses* and Virgil's fourth Eclogue—Ovid
giving an account of the Golden Age, "when men of their own
accord, without threat of punishment, without laws, maintained
good faith and did what was right," while Virgil foretold that
age's return through the birth of a divine child who would rein-
augurate the happy reign of heaven on earth.

Despite the passage of centuries between Hesiod's *Works and
Days* and the various permutations of Golden Age lore that follow,
its basic picture of humanity in bliss remains amazingly intact, like
a dream that refuses to go away. With its portrait of social well-
being undisturbed by nature's resistance or human perversity,
Kronos' kingdom constitutes an abiding fantasy of our fulfillment
as imagined from the perspective of Iron—a feat of the imagination's "alchemical" transformation. But locked within Hesiod's
impossible dream of bodies that do not age, or suffer pain, or
experience a mortal's death, there is at base a hard notion of what

constitutes human flourishing. For when we eliminate the obviously mythic elements of Hesiod's account, what we find is
something like the following "platform": labor without suffering,
pleasure in corporate activity and festival, a shared abundance of
material goods, an ease of existence befitting the gods. We find,
in other words, goals that exemplify utopian imagining from
Thomas More's originating work, to Karl Marx's vision of a classless society, to the various communitarian experiments of the
1960's. Even Hesiod's idea of a succession of historical ages
devolving from the "golden generation" has its equivalent in the
secular utopian thinkers of the eighteenth and nineteenth centuries, with their positing of an initial period of bliss followed by
a long interim of misery, and concluded in the founding of utopia
with its restitution of earthly happiness. King Kronos awaits his
second coming.

Like any other educated man in the sixteenth century,
Thomas More had at his disposal this pagan tradition of a "prelap-
sarian" world that could be enjoyed in memory, as in Ovid's
Metamorphoses, or even, as Virgil suggests in his Eclogue, anticipated in the future. Yet More's thinking was inevitably formed
by that other account of human origins that claimed not only his
fancy, but his belief. I am referring, of course, to the Bible's
perspective on human flourishing, both in the beginning and at
the end of history, as it unfolds in the course of Scripture from
Genesis to Revelation. While sharing certain superficial resem-
blances with the pagan account of human origins, it tells its own
distinctive (and at times radically different) story. Thus utopia
inherits two worlds of discourse on the ideal, a double legacy that
only serves to compound its air of ambivalence. Just as More's
pun signifies the "good place" and "no place" at one and the same
time, so too the concept of utopia draws on mutually contradictory notions of the happy life. At least in its beginning, it wants
to be pagan and Christian at once—a very uneasy and unsettling
mix, as the history of utopian thought since the sixteenth century
plainly demonstrates.

Our sense of this difficulty is heightened when we compare
Scripture's perspective on human fulfillment with the rather
different one offered by *Utopia*'s most important precursor text—
the work which More emulated even as he sought to supercede
it—the *Republic*. Plato was not concerned with the myth of

original human happiness; he writes instead about the possibility
of a rational political order in which the less fantastic aspects of
King Kronos' reign find their equivalent in an ideal city in which
justice obtains and the good finds its corporate human realization.
In juxtaposing biblical teaching and Platonic speculation, I want
to suggest the complex influence that makes utopia at once so
dynamic and so ambivalent an enterprise. Once this double line
of descent is clarified, we will be in a better position to get closer
to the actual "nowheres" that take up the remainder of this book,
constructed as they are either with an eye towards Scripture or
towards Plato. As we shall see, it is perhaps only More who
manages to keep utopia's contradictions in concord, giving both
lines of inheritance their due.

When we turn to the first chapters of the book of Genesis,
what we find in the Garden of Eden is not so much the recollection of a Golden Age as a masterpiece of withheld information:
a perfect *mystery*. To be sure, in the brief description offered
by Genesis 2 there is everything about the place itself to thrill the
desert imagination that conceived it: fertile soil loaded with gold
and precious stones, four irrigating rivers, an abundance of trees
"pleasant to the sight and good for food," delicate mists in place
of violent rainstorms, and animals who do their best to be
"helpers." The Lord God plants a garden in Eden which is *eden*
("bliss") indeed.

But when we attempt to extrapolate what human life was
actually like there—when we look for models of perfect social
organization—we find ourselves standing before a wall of silence.
The Yahwist's narrative raises many more questions about our
original state than it ever answers; it leaves us "stalled" in speculation. With only the rather bare text of Genesis as testimony, we
are left with the knowledge that God supplied the conditions of
human flourishing in the beginning, but after the Fall kept them
hidden and enclosed within the Garden's precinct, unavailable to
those who had never been there. Lacking the details offered by
Hesiod or Ovid in their evocations of a life without pain or conflict, the best we can manage with our biblical source is an act of
imaginative recovery. We can, that is, roll back the curses that
fall upon Adam and Eve after their eating of the forbidden fruit
and follow them out of the Garden and into the fallen world. In
other words, the reader must attempt to discover humanity's lost

bliss through a "negation of the negative in human existence," converting the several "dooms" pronounced by God in Genesis 3 into the largely unspecified joys of Eden.

What we find through a feat of reconstruction is something like the following: an earth that need not be struggled against, a body that suffers no pain, a harmonious relationship between the sexes, easy childbirth, work without the onerous burden of labor, an intimate communication with a God who walks in the Garden in the cool of the day, conversing with creatures who were made both to share in and enjoy such talk. What we get from such an exercise, therefore, are hints of a paradise irretrievably lost. And indeed it is an overwhelming sense of this loss that finally claims our attention. For instead of some Semitic version of the Age of Kronos, lovingly detailed in all its paradisical luxuries and benefits, Genesis focuses our concern on the question of obedience to God and the consequences of its rupture. It leaves us, in other words, with very little sense of the pleasures of the place, confronting the reader instead with the stark realization of human sin.

A shadow stretches outward from Eden that casts its darkness over every subsequent instance of human association, from the founding of the first city by the murderer Cain, to Babel's attempt to take heaven by storm, to the murmurings and apostacies that keep Israel wandering for forty years in the wilderness. With the settlement in the land of milk and honey, however, the lost ideal of the Garden reappears in another form as Zion. An image of human fulfillment fostered by the Davidic monarchy and centered on the city of Jerusalem, the desire for Zion expresses the hope that God might once more be present to the earth. Through the rule of a human king, Yahweh might extend the heavenly reign of justice and righteousness to a chosen people.

> For the Lord has chosen Zion;
>   he has desired it for his habitation:
> 'This is my resting place for ever;
>   here I will dwell, for I have desired it.
> I will abundantly bless her provisions;
>   I will satisfy her poor with bread.'
>   (Ps. 132: 13-18)

Whereas in Genesis 2 we are told that occasionally God would

walk with Adam and Eve in the cool of the day, the psalm proclaims that the Lord will make Jerusalem his "resting place
forever." This choice of habitation has, of course, the most profound implications for Israel. For with God's commitment to
dwell in the midst of a particular human community is joined the
promise to "bless," "satisfy," "clothe" and "make rejoice": the
promise that Zion will become, so to speak, a national Eden.
Furthermore, it is through the person of the king that heaven is
to make itself felt on earth, as the curse of postlapsarian life is
redeemed by acts of restoration and mercy, so that "the moun-
tains bear prosperity for the people, and the hills, in righteousness" (Ps 72:3). Because of God's promise to Zion, which stands
to reverse the ancient exile from earthly joy suffered since the
expulsion from Eden, the experience of happy days, so distant in
memory, shall be Israel's once again.

This confident identification of Jerusalem with "the city of
our God" (Ps. 48.1) did not go uncriticized. Isaiah for one saw in
the proclamations of Zion a pious cover-up, the self-congratulation
of a "sinful nation, a people laden with iniquity" (Is. 1.4). Nor
could it survive intact the traumas of history, which witnessed the
destruction of temple and monarchy alike as well as the mass
deportation of God's elect to Babylon. The Lord's chosen "good
place" had become quite literally no place at all—a transformation
which might be assumed to have destroyed all sense of Zion as
being anything more than an exploded fantasy. And yet, despite
the difficulty of singing the Lord's song in a strange land, it was
precisely the vision of Jerusalem as Zion, the "citadel" of God on
earth, that gave this exiled people hope. It enabled them to hold
on to the future and therefore survive the vicissitudes of the
present. For some, this hope was placed quite concretely in a
restoration of the earthly kingdom and temple cult that had been
lost; for others, however, it was in a fuller manifestation of justice
and righteousness than had ever been realized in the past. In
their longing Zion became an eschatological reality standing on the
far shore of possibility—a "nowhere" that transcended the horizontal realizations of politics and history, whose promise of a
"good place" on earth represented a future manifestation of God's
will. The Lord would renew the world, with Jerusalem "a rejoic-
ing" and the law of the Garden restored:

> The wolf and the lamb shall feed together,
>   the lion shall eat straw like the ox;
>   and dust shall be the serpent's food.
> They shall not hurt or destroy in all my
>   holy mountain.
>
>   (Is. 65: 25)

It is in the prophets of Israel that we best can find the delicate balance between a call to bring about social justice and amelioration within the human community—what Tillich speaks of as the partial transcendence of utopia in the political and social sense—and, on the other hand, the call to expect something to be given by God. Thus, in the one case, we work to remove what Isaiah calls "the reproach of the people" through acts of justice, while in the other, we accept the removal of reproach as an act ultimately beyond our powers, resting in some future revelation or "uncovering" (*apokalyptein*) of God's will for the world. A similar balance is struck by Jesus in his proclamation of the kingdom of heaven. Although his teaching was unmistakably "in" the world, with its advocacy of the traditional prophetic themes of social justice and personal righteousness, it was definitely not "of it." Rejecting all forms of political power and every attempt to rebuild an earthly Zion in his own image and likeness, Jesus bore witness to a kingdom that would be borne out and enacted in the corporate life of the redeemed community, and yet which was still to come. We get some sense of it, at least as it can be imagined now, in the Beatitudes that preface Matthew's account of the Sermon on the Mount—an ideal of humanity as it might be under the rule of God. In frequently asking his listeners to imagine what the kingdom of heaven was "like," Jesus was also introducing them to a notion of community that was unlike anything they knew, but whose transforming presence was already at work in their midst. He asked them to press forward, in other words, toward what finally would be *given* to them.

The early church heard this message as an invitation to become members incorporate in a new creation, a living temple—a profoundly organic sense of communal involvement which St. Paul could speak of as the body of Christ. In daily life these Christians might render unto Caesar the appropriate tribute and acknowledge the governing authorities, but their real locus of identity would be elsewhere. Their community might occasionally defy established social norm (as in the Jerusalem church, where all things were held in common—Acts 2:44, 4:32), but more importantly it opened to its baptized "citizens" a world of renewed minds and transformed relationships—a peaceable kingdom no less striking than Isaiah's vision of lion and lamb. "For as many of you as were baptized into Christ have put on Christ. There is neither Jew nor Greek, there is neither slave nor free, there is neither male nor female; for you are all one in Christ" (Gal. 3:27-28).

The biblical rearrangement of traditional hierarchy into a transcendent equality of persons united "in Christ" cannot be construed as a program for social reorganization, although utopian thinkers in later ages will take it as a warrant for radical political change. It is, however, a vision of reality not only as it may be experienced more fully in the last days, but as it can already be glimpsed now in the community of the faithful, before that ultimate transformation of history into what eye has not seen, nor ear heard, nor mortal mind conceived. It is a declaration of reality known only imperfectly in history, but one which is made in anticipation of that full redemption of the world toward which the whole creation has groaned in travail since the beginning. So it is only fitting that when the Bible offers its ultimate image of perfection in the final chapters of Revelation, we should find there a recapitulation of the two great images of human flourishing that the Old Testament passes on to the New. Once again we are given the primordial Garden, with its tree of life and flowing rivers. But now the green oasis that was planted by God somewhere "in the east" is seen at the heart of a splendid and altogether transcendent Zion. It is, therefore, a composite image of scriptural beatitude—an image of Garden *and* City—which St. John the Divine sees at the climax of his apocalyptic vision descending from heaven like a bride to a wedding of the new heaven and the new earth:

> and I heard a loud voice from the throne saying,
> 'Behold, the dwelling of God is with men. He will dwell
> with them, and they shall be his people, and God
> himself will be with them; he will wipe away every tear
> from their eyes, and death shall be no more, neither

shall there be mourning nor crying nor pain any more,
for the former things have passed away.'
(Rev. 21: 1-4)

Radiant, open to all nations and transparent to God's glory, the
New Jerusalem is a vindication of all the promises made to Zion
and long buried under centuries of apostasy, destruction and
shattered hopes. This is the "good place" where God at last
resides with us, in which all the "former things" that have plagued
both individual and community since Eden have passed away.

But just as we were forced in Genesis to reverse the curses
levelled against Adam and Eve in order to glimpse what their pre-
lapsarian life might have been, so here we can enter vicariously
into the joy of the holy city only by reimagining our life here,
among the "former things." We have to cancel the negatives in
human existence (tears, pain, mourning, death) to discover some
inkling of the final beatitude for which we were intended from the
beginning. Yet how it is that the blessed will live together—how
"God himself will be with them"—remains inscrutable. All we
have is a blank page for the imagination to trespass upon. Because
the truth of the matter is that the Bible always presents its para-
digms of bliss as standing *outside* our historical frame of reference,
either before human existence as we know it or after the apocalypse ushers in that new heaven and new earth we cannot imagine.

Despite our constant temptation to force an earthly Jerusalem
into the mold of the heavenly Zion, the hope of human fulfillment
lies always beyond days and years, in a fullness of time that
transcends time as we know it. Whether we are considering the
garden of Genesis or the holy city of Revelation, the place of full
human happiness is always presented as a gift from God and not
as a human achievement. Thus, in the beginning paradise is
planted for humankind "in the east"; in the end it descends from
God out of heaven "as a bride adorned for her husband." In
either case, it is not constructed by human beings according to
what they think is meet and right. No, our fulfillment as a race is
something revealed and offered by God and God alone. As a
testimony both to our finitude and our sinfulness, the Scripture
claims that, try as we will, we cannot in the end either "make" or
perfect ourselves. Our identity, like our needs, can only be fully
satisfied elsewhere, by someone else.

Given the start-to-finish consistency of this biblical position, it is interesting to note how difficult it has been for Christian culture to leave the notion of a perfect place at that—in God's hands. Apparently the myth of heaven on earth is one that dies hard, a loss that we cannot sustain for very long. Right up into the fifteenth century and among the most sophisticated of Europeans, there remained a persistent belief in a terrestrial Garden of Eden, the original "good place" as yet undiscovered by sinful humanity, but nonetheless quite clearly marked on all the old maps of the world as standing at the farthest reaches of the east. To be sure, the terrestrial paradise would be empty of inhabitants and strictly off-limits to mortals; still, it was commonly held to be located at some point on the earth—a place for the imagination to fancy and (at least in daydream) to rein-habit. Or even, perhaps, to stumble upon. No less experienced a traveller than Christopher Columbus thought he had discovered its site in 1498 when, poised at the mouth of the Orinoco River in what is now the territory of Brazil—and seeing four tributary rivers, lush foliage, abundant gold and precious stones in the rich earth—he made the quite understandable assumption that he had wandered onto the threshhold of Eden. It was then, out of fear of trespassing on the sacred soil, that he fled north immediately to take refuge elsewhere—on the safe (if postlapsarian) island of Hispaniola.[5]

But far more important than this fascination with the actual whereabouts of Eden was the millenarian belief that after an immense historical catastrophe, perfection would come and totally transform the order of terrestrial life. After his Second Coming, Christ would establish a messianic kingdom on the earth and reign over it for a thousand years before the Day of Judgment. As Norman Cohn traces in *The Pursuit of the Millenium*, there was much speculation among the church fathers as to what this kingdom would actually be like.[6] Given the Bible's great silence in these matters, it was inevitable that they should find their rhetoric outside the Scriptures. Understandably, given their "classical" educations, the Fathers turned to the language of Hesiod, Virgil, and Ovid to describe the delights that awaited the faithful in Christ's millenium. And so Lactantius in the fourth century, actively seeking pagan converts to Christianity, advertises to his audience that heaven on earth which is "soon" to come once Christ returns: "Then the rain of blessing shall descend from God morning and evening, and the earth shall bear all fruits without man's labours. Honey in abundance shall drip from the rocks, fountains of milk and wine shall burst forth. The beasts of the forests shall put away their wildness and become tame."[7] What we find in this prophetic fantasy is the eschatological vision of Isaiah, crossed with the language of the Promised Land, and then raised to the luxuriant heights of the *Metamorphoses*. It was exactly this kind of millenarian fantasy that Augustine opposed in his *City of God*, and with a polemical line that soon became Catholic orthodoxy. For Augustine the events foretold in the book of Revelation were a spiritual allegory of what had already come to pass. The millenium had been inaugurated by the birth of Christianity and could already be experienced in the life of the church as it spread its influence throughout the Roman empire and leavened the lump of sinful humanity.

Having said this, Augustine would not go on to equate the church on earth with the City of God. No, the church was a pilgrim body—the *civitas peregrina*—and a tent of meeting rather than the temple itself. Precisely because of this provisional status, its mission in the world was to herald and prepare for that perfect kingdom which was the true seat of human fulfillment: Jerusalem, "above and free," the eternal reality of which any earthly community, whatever its sanctity, could only be considered a type or shadow. To pray for that kingdom, as the pilgrim church is constantly bid to do, is not to assume we will greet it with mortal eyes, let alone have a share in its construction. Its shining towers stand on the far side of death, across that great gulf fixed between earth and heaven.

Despite the official victory of Augustine's position on these matters, millenarian hopes have continued to spring up—perhaps in recognition of a legitimate need for earthly fulfillment that refuses deferment to another world, which requires an apocalypse *now*. Groups throughout the history of Christian culture have waited in earnest expectation for the advent of the kingdom of heaven to transform earthly society "from within." Think, for example, of the twelfth-century abbot Joachim of Fiore and his prophecy of the coming Reign of the Holy Ghost (an era when "we shall not be what we have been, but we shall begin to be other"), or of the Anabaptist circle of the fifteenth-century Thomas Müntzer and his proclamation of an egalitarian brotherhood, or of the nineteenth-century community founded by George Rapp in New Harmony, Indiana, which assumed it could not only anticipate Christ's millenial reign, but actually bring it to pass.

Although the monastic life is not in any sense a millenarian experiment, it is tempting to consider its reorganization of secular existence along the lines of the City of God as another attempt to bring heaven down to earth. This association of the monastery with an effort to construct an ideal "good place" where human beings might flourish as God intended would also seem to be borne out by the famous ninth-century plan for a model Benedictine community at St. Gall.[8] At first glance it looks like a blueprint for a Christian utopia, an anticipation of the millenial kingdom of Christ. Separated from the rest of the world to the greatest degree possible, almost autonomous within the circuit of its projected walls, the Plan of St. Gall represents a vision of social order strictly governed by religious rule and under the strict administration of a "father in God," the abbot. It offers its inhabitants a total reorientation of profane existence. Time and space, work and rest, every kind of personal interaction is to be regulated down to the least detail by a notion of human flourishing that places the worship of God at both center and circumference of daily life. The Plan of St. Gall would seem to be nothing less than a simulacrum of the divine order on earth—a translation of an entirely spiritual realm into "flesh"—as cloister garden and abbey church mimic in their terrestrial ways the New Jerusalem of Revelation 21-22.

But it is precisely this element of mimicry that must be remembered when considering the utopian dimensions of monasticism. For if the Plan of St. Gall represents a kind of perfection, the monastery itself was never confused with the ideal toward which it pointed. For all its beautiful symmetries of construction and activity, for all the rounds of worship that would seem to spirit the community out of this world, the monastery understood itself as a place established in order to assist its members in their struggle against the world, the flesh, and the devil. It was never conceived as anything more than a provisional or penultimate ideal; like all things earthly it too would pass away at the advent of something better. Despite the fortress-like appearance of the monastic enclosure, it was merely the departure point for a

spiritual pilgrimage, the starting-line of a journey whose destination lay outside its walls and hours of prayer, in a heavenly
mansion which God, and God alone, had prepared for eternity.
The truly happy life toward which the monastery pointed its
pilgrim-citizens awaited the further disclosure of paradise.

* * *

What we have traced above is one side of utopia's family tree.
Despite the constant temptation to locate Zion in the here and
now, or to find the millenium anticipated in some new regime of
living, the biblical influence on utopian imagining understands
human fulfillment primarily to lie beyond our achievement and
therefore to rest in other hands. If never properly disengaged
from the needs of the world, it is still otherworldly in its sense of
our origins and destiny, in its acknowledgement that our ultimate
happiness lies hidden in God and therefore beyond what we can
either desire or deserve. For this reason the Bible proclaims the
"good place" of all our longing to be a kingdom that is nowhere
on earth, never securely within our grasp, incapable of concrete
realization given the limitations of our understanding as well as of
our sinfulness. The distinctly Christian vision of utopia, therefore,
is an image of hope.

But the biblical witness is only one side of utopia's story—and
not the major one at that. Far more influential in the development of utopian imagining is the influence that descended to
Thomas More from ancient Greece and, in particular, from the
thought world of Plato's *Republic*. Instead of a dream or vision,
it offers a goal; instead of a kingdom to come, it proposes an ideal
communal order which purports to be capable of realization in the
here and now. Reason and will applied to the human situation
bring about the happy life, without any notion of grace or divine
empowerment. Confident about the possibility of our getting it
right after all, Plato joins an interest in the actual structures and
functions of society to a faith in the power of human beings to
bring about their own fulfillment. In lieu of utopia as God's
deliverance of us, he offers us hope in our own strength. We have
it of ourselves to help ourselves.

Like many another utopian thinker, Plato turned his imagination to the overhaul of society out of a combination of frustration

and hope. Disgusted by the corruption of his own fifth century
Athens—and perhaps most especially by the "revolutionary"
reforms that made ousted regimes appear in comparison like an
age of gold—he intended as a young man to enter the arena of
politics and bring about some positive change. With the execution
of Socrates on trumped-up charges of "impiety," however, he
despaired over the possibility that intelligence and integrity could
even survive within the political sphere, so venal and stupid were
the powers that be. As he says in the autobiographical terms of
his Seventh Letter, "The troubles of mankind will never cease
until either true and genuine philosophers attain political power or
the rulers of states by some disposition of providence become
genuine philosophers."9

To this end Plato founded the Academy in Athens expressly in
hope of training the kind of philosophic statesman it would take
to reorder what the Seventh Letter speaks of as the "dizzy spec-
tacle of universal confusion." It was in the heady atmosphere of
this school in its early and most optimistic days (c. 380 B.C.E.),
in a setting where it was possible to think that education might
hold the key to the future, that the dialogue of the *Republic* came
into being. Indeed, the *Republic* itself can be seen as a statement
of what the Academy set about to achieve: the transformation of
the actual political order by a class of rulers able to take a city no
more virtuous or ideal than Athens and then to recast its institutions and customs in the image of justice. Without recourse to
any notion of divine intervention, with its implantation of a new
heart and a new mind in an old humanity, Plato was interested in
the possibility of changing life as we know it not by mass conversion, but by a rational reordering of priorities and ideals. The
state is like a body, capable of health just as it is liable to disease.
What matters is that we learn the medicine of statecraft, that we
keep an eye on the well-being of the total organism—and then, of
course, that we follow doctor's orders. The secret of good health
lies in abiding by what is prescribed.

More manifesto than specific plan, more program of education
than portrait of the ideal state, the *Republic* offers a number of
priorities and assumptions about the constitution of the "good
place" that eventually become, as we shall see, the almost universal possession of subsequent utopian thought. In dramatic
contrast to the dominant tradition of Scripture, with its emphasis

on the gift of God's kingdom as the ultimate source of human fulfillment, Plato's preoccupation is with the education of leadership—the cultivation of persons who will be able to translate heavenly forms of justice into a just social and political order.

For this reason his effort is toward the realization of a class of rulers or guardians who would know and love the truth, could distinguish between true needs and false, and who would dedicate themselves to strive for the happiness of the whole state rather than the advancement of their private interests. Such rulers were to be so regulated in their development, both through a process of eugenic breeding and through the most careful program of education, that they should be capable of envisioning accurately a truly just society.

What that ideal republic would look like is something Plato does not reveal in any detail. He imagines three classes of people: a majority of farmers and artisans, a much smaller number of administrators or guardians of the social order, and a tiny group of philosopher-rulers to envision the whole. Such classes are not hereditary but reapportioned generation after generation, so that those with natural gifts for production, administration, and reason (corresponding to the three parts of the soul) are channeled in the direction of their gift. Everyone has a specific role to play which, while expressive of individual ability, is oriented toward the good of the whole social organism. The tempering or "justification" of society, then, consists in each person's living in terms of the corporate well-being. The private, as such, has ceased to exist. Such a world, moreover, is locked into place by common consent—a rigid hierarchy of class and value, maintaining (as far as might be possible in a world of flux and instability) an order of earthly organization that approximates the immutability of the heavens.

All of this would "work," finally, because supreme authority is intended to rest with those who have both the vision and virtue to exercise such power with equity—to be tyrants of wisdom. In the ideal republic, therefore, the *philosopher* is king. And because this lofty position serves as the keystone of the entire structure, Plato—as one might expect of the founding father of an Academy devoted expressly to cultivating the brightest and best—is at pains to insure that only the finest examples of humanity present themselves for the office. Nothing is left to chance. The republic is always searching out its youngest generation, looking for the male or female children who show a predisposition to search for the higher reaches of reason. Those who pass muster are rigorously educated in a full sequence of studies, a course of enlightenment that culminates in the dialectic of philosophy, and with it the contemplation of the Good. Cut off from the distractions of family and possessions, the philosophers are to live in such a way that their individuality merges with the state. All they have, in other words, is the common wealth. With private property and intense intimate relationships cast aside, they are free to dedicate their lives to an unhampered knowledge of the Good, not for private enlightenment, but for the benefit of others. They are to shape their society in the image and likeness of eternal truths that the human community might stand in harmony with the perfect working of the universe.

We search in vain throughout Plato's discussion for any doubt as to whether the Good can be known reliably, or whether knowledge of it would necessarily lead to righteousness. The exalted spirits of the philosophical ruling class seem a world away from St. Paul's predicament, "I can will what is right, but I cannot do it" (Rom. 7:18). "Sin," if we can use that term, seems a weakness of the lower classes. In the upper reaches of republican society, however, confidence reigns supreme in the power of human reason to grasp reality and to share its vision with those of lesser gifts. Philosophers always know best. Like gods they have grasped the true pattern of truth, and have apprehended exactly what it would take to bring this ragged mess in which we live into the clean shape of social perfection.

There is no *Realpolitik* in the *Republic*, no handbook of advice for how to bring about a revolution of the Good in human affairs. But in a passage found in VI.500, in which the philosopher-king is presented metaphorically as an artist working over his material, we are given some sense of how Plato saw the task in hand. It is a portrait of the utopian as a human god, bringing the "good place" into being by quasi-divine fiat.

> He will take society and human character as his canvas, and begin by scraping it clean. That is no easy matter; but, as you know, unlike other reformers, he will not consent to take in hand either an individual or

> a state or to draft laws, until he is given a clean surface
> to work on, or has cleansed it himself . . . . Combining
> [the] various elements of social life as a painter mixes
> his colours, he will reproduce the complexion of true
> humanity, guided by that divine pattern whose likeness
> Homer saw in the men he called godlike. He will rub
> out and paint in again this or that feature, until he has
> produced, so far as may be, a type of human character
> that heaven can approve.[10]

To read this passage is to contemplate an image of the Demiurge
at work. It is also an extremely vivid portrayal of utopia's impulse
to remake the world, as breathtaking in its scope as it is frightening to contemplate. There is so much power and sheer self-
assurance here! Not only does the philosopher know the model
from which he will paint ("the ideals of justice, goodness, temperance, and the rest"), not only can he reproduce an earthly copy of
those ideals ("true humanity"), but the human beings who are his
canvas, brushstroke and color will conform entirely to his image
of them—or run the risk of being "rubbed out"! He is their
creator, and what their destiny would seem to be is, quite simply,
the fulfillment of *his* terms of creation. He is to rejoice in the
work of his hands, It is their job to conform to the divine pattern
which he, and he alone, has seen. They are utterly his to work
on.

This benign but essentially totalitarian dream expresses in a
dramatic way the driving impulse which is more or less hidden
within every attempt to make utopia happen: the impulse to
create a new heaven and a new earth. Missing from the account is
any clear sense of what it would take to bring the just society
about, or what would happen to those who declined to enjoy its
perfection, or what the reign of reason would mean for a people
that has always cherished its idiosyncrasies and freedom to step
out of line. Plato simply avers that once the philosopher demonstrates his visionary wares—or, more likely still, has the power to
enforce them absolutely—"he will not lack the skill to produce
such counterparts of temperance, justice, and all the virtues as can
exist in ordinary men." One way or another, the people will
invariably see it his way, and in time he will get it right after all.

At the conclusion of *Republic* VI.500, Plato's spokesman says,

"We have, I believe, sufficiently shown that our plan, if practicable, is the best. So, to conclude: our institutions would be the best, if they could be realized, and to realize them, though hard, is not impossible." Indeed, in a subsequent dialogue, the *Critias*, Plato proposed through his title character to describe how an ideal city had once existed in ancient Athens, as if in testimony to the proposition that the ideal was, after all, capable of actual historical realization. Judging by the extant texts of that dialogue, Plato never made good on his bargain. Nor were his attempts to turn the tyrant of Sicily into a philosopher-king anything more than a disaster—and one from which he only narrowly escaped with his life. But for all this failure and incompletion, what he undoubtedly bequeathed to Western culture was a conviction that the ideal society was a feasible reality, a goal within the grasp of reason and human resolve. There was no inherent reason why a new creation could not replace the old, except that instead of descending as St. John the Divine saw it, from the hand of God, it would come to earth within the mind of the philosopher. All that was lacking was power to implement the plan.

As we turn in the following chapters to consider some concrete instances of utopian imagining, what we will need to keep in mind is the uneasy fit between a biblical notion of human fulfillment as God's gift and, on the other hand, a classical belief in an ideal order on earth, where human beings can find their fulfillment in a world of their own making. The fantasy of utopia emerged from this complex history at a time when these two contradictory notions seemed capable, if not of resolution, then at least of intimate conversation. As we see in many works of the Renaissance imagination—whether in Filarete's designs for a perfectly proportioned city, or in authors like More who tried to complete the *Republic's* unfinished business—it was a moment in Christian culture when the Fall did not seem so powerful as to prevent humanity from bringing earthly communities more in line with an ideal. Some harmonization of Christ and Apollo was possible. After all, we had an almost infinite capacity to choose the self we would become, to be the angel as well as the beast. Why not, then, a newer Jerusalem on earth—a commonwealth in which we might explore one of God's greatest gifts to humanity, the ability to change and improve the world into which we were born?

This is the question which More poses in the early sixteenth century and which appears again and again—although with a less orthodox formulation in subsequent ages, when God and the gift of the kingdom cease to be the subject of much serious utopian consideration. Nonetheless the question of humanity's power to transform and improve will continue to confront us as we see the joint heirs of both Scripture and *Republic* attempt to imagine a world in which we can find ourselves truly at home, fulfilling the promise of earthly happiness that utopia has always maintained is our destiny. Why *shouldn't* Zion haste?

a happy commonwealth

It may be that every breakthrough of the imagination awaits its
fullness of time, that moment when the inchoate ruminations of
the past suddenly take shape and give substance to what had been
for ages only an unexpressed dream. So it was with utopia.
Plato had failed to picture it in the *Republic* and subsequent
centuries could no more bring the vision into focus than he—but
in 1516 Thomas More opened up a territory that has never been
deserted since. In the two thousand years that stretch between
Plato and More there had been a great deal of thought about the
nature of the "good place" of human flourishing, as existing either
at some point in the distant past (as in Plutarch's recreation of
Solon's Athens in his *Parallel Lives*), or, according to mainstream
Christianity, in the paradise of eternity. For centuries the imagination of the West was kept busy recreating ancient history or
anticipating the future, but what it could not do was take charge
of the here and now. It could not describe the conditions of
human fulfillment as they might exist on the earth as we know it.

This situation changed in the course of the Renaissance, when
a rediscovery of Hellenic culture—and specifically of the *Republic*,
published in Ficino's Latin translation of 1484—turned the attention of humanist scholars to an authoritative text that not only
took the earthly commonwealth very seriously, but had as one of
its objectives the positive transformation of the political and social
order. With the enticing possibility of actually doing something
with the earth, conditions were ripe for the birth of utopia, for
imagining how much more closely to the good our own collective
portrait might be drawn. This is not to say that notions of Plato's
republic replaced a concern with the kingdom of heaven, or that
the dividing line between paradise and polis had been blurred
beyond recognition. These were developments to occur centuries
later. But it is to suggest that learned Christians began to hear the
teachings of the kingdom with new ears, as if the gospel promise

of renewal might pertain not only to the state of the soul after death, or to the cosmos after apocalypse, but to a renewed life within the earthly city itself.[11]

Of course the Christian humanists of whom I am speaking understood that the ancients spoke without the benefit of divine revelation and therefore fell short of the ultimate truth. At the same time they were thought to have spoken truly, sometimes covertly in symbol and enigma, sometimes more directly, about a variety of temporal concerns which by the sixteenth century seemed supremely compatible with the thrust of Christian teaching. For many humanists it was apparent that Jerusalem stood to learn a great deal from Athens—if not about the substance of the faith, then at least about the feasibility of living decently within the terrestrial order. Plato had something to teach not only about things transcendent or metaphysical, but also about the place of wisdom in the practical world of politics.

A quintessential expression of the Renaissance humanism that was to be so formative in More's intellectual development—and in so many ways exemplifies the spirit of all utopian thought—is Pico della Mirandola's "Oration," commonly subtitled "On the Dignity of Man."[12] Written in 1486 by a twenty-four year old prodigy, the work is an extraordinary synthesis of east and west, Plato and Aristotle, Hebrew and Christian, Moslem and pagan—"as both Moses and Timaeus witness." But more striking than its syncretism is the oration's theory of human nature, which seemed to articulate for Pico's contemporaries a new (and very attractive) attitude toward ourselves and the multitudinous possibilities that lie before us. Perhaps more than anything else it was Pico's sublimely Platonic reappraisal of human nature, with both its astonishing optimism about human potential and its very limited notion of human sin, that accounted for the work's immense popularity and wide translation. More clearly than any other single Renaissance text, it shows us the spiritual climate in which utopian imagination would come to fruition.

Pico della Mirandola was not a utopian strategist. Yet the implications of his passionately inspirational text help suggest not only why this period saw the birth of utopia, but what notion of human being underlies the vision of an ideal earthly commonwealth. To begin with, his oration proclaims us to be creatures

who are by nature infinitely elastic, possessed of a self that can
stretch from the lower depths up to the heavens. Pico's emphasis
is on the self-transcendence and self-fashioning of the *individual*,
an activity one imagines being performed alone, in the seclusion of
a private study, by persons of extraordinary spiritual refinement.
But it is equally possible to consider this capacity for change in its
larger (and corporate) dimension, as an indication of our capacity
to be molded en masse. Pico's theory of human nature can, in
other words, be taken out of the private study and into the market
place and assembly hall. There it shows us to be creatures who
can be turned into almost anything—for better or for worse. Just
as the fact of our indeterminacy proclaims at once the freedom
and the responsibility of individuals to mold themselves, so too it
opens up an opportunity for someone else to do it for them. For
while we as moral "chameleons" are free to transform ourselves
into angels or beasts, we are also radically susceptible to *being*
transformed into someone else's vision of us—like the artistic
"materials" worked over with such care by Plato's philosopher-
king. In some sense, then, our nature is up for grabs. We can
become something quite other than what we are; our essence is
mutable, and so too, by implication, are the societies in which we
live.

Second, it is through education in the humanities—and, in
particular, through the dialectic of philosophy—that we are
capable of positive transformation. Again, Pico is speaking for
and about the individual, as well as about himself and his own
intense dedication to learning. But his emphasis on the priority
of education in the transformation of the self sounds a note
that not only picks up on Plato's dominant theme in the *Republic*,
but is also echoed throughout the long course of utopian imagining. Education holds the key to the future. It is the means by
which malleable creatures are shaped into finer configurations
of the self, closer approximations of the ideal. For Pico education is also the means of social renewal, enabling the commonwealth to resist the downward pull of destructive impulses and
fight the good fight against its own baser instincts. For if an
individual can learn to settle for nothing less than the angel
within, why not the body politic itself?

Finally, by entertaining Pico's propositions about human
nature in their full social dimension, we are brought to the

question that all utopias raise and then just as inevitably answer—in the affirmative. Given the indeterminacy of human nature, and its ability to be shaped for good as well as for ill, is there a specific plan which can be followed, some principle of social reorganization by which the angel can be given his due and the beast left behind? Or, to use the theatrical metaphor with which Pico opens his oration, is there a particular kind of political "stage" on which we can be so inspired by the ideal setting that each and every one of us becomes a superb actor? With these questions once more in the air, we are ready for utopia's response.

* * *

By New Year's Day 1505, less than a decade after Pico's death, Thomas More completed a translation of Giovanni Francesco's *Vita Pici* and presented it as a gift to a newly-professed Poor Clare under the title, *Life of John Picus, Erle of Myrandula*.[13] It was a work that emphasized the extraordinary order of events which overtook Pico upon his first promulgation of the "dignity of man." Accused of heresy, he took refuge in Florence at the Platonic Academy under the protection of Lorenzo de'Medici. There he was converted to an austere notion of the Christian life by Savanarola's fire-and-brimstone preaching and declared his desire to follow Christ by becoming a mendicant friar, "bare fote walkynge about the worlde in every town and castel." He died before finally resolving to live this life of worldly renunciation.

What More translated, in effect, was the account of a heady Platonist who, under the pressure of reality, realized the folly of his "hye mynde and proud purpose." Indeed, the true story of Pico's dramatic conversion to a radical sense of human limitation and sinfulness, expressed in the grim terms of Savonarola's religion, inevitably throws the exuberance of the Oration into suspicion, as if it were no more than the giddy intellectual flight of a very young man carried away with fancy ideas untested by experience. The biography More translated in effect exposed the "dignity of man" to be a house of cards ready for a fall. It was a "life" meant to encourage a new Poor Clare in her resolve to abandon the world, and a cautionary tale for More himself to ponder. After all, he was a man who had recently rejected the cloister in favor of marriage and an active legal and professional

life in the city of London. He had devoted much of his youth
to the same *studia humanistica* which Pico had ended up viewing
with wariness as "ful of pride, desirous of glorie and mannes
praise."

And yet the translator of this *Life of John Picus*, who had a
few years earlier dazzled the "reverend Fathers" of London with
his learned lectures on Augustine's *De civitate Dei*, was in ten
year's time to produce the first fruits of what would prove to be a
long utopian harvest—a portrait of transformed human community which the first (1516) edition of *Utopia* is proud to proclaim
"a rival of Plato's republic, and perhaps even a victor over it."
The process by which More came to write his book seems to have
followed the rough outline of my own less productive experience
in the Berkshire hills: a conversation with a friend about how bad
things are, followed by a more or less serious vision of how everything in society might be better. In 1515 a very preoccupied
man—lawyer, under-sheriff of London, advocate of the English
cloth industry abroad and conscientious *pater familias* at home—
found himself with the utterly unaccustomed luxury of free
time. Appointed by Henry VIII as ambassador in negotiations
between England and the Continent over what *Utopia* itself calls
"certain weighty matters," More and his companions discovered
after two months of talks that they were at a stalemate. It lasted
all of three months, and so, unable to return home but with
relatively little to do, More went to Antwerp for a visit with a
humanist friend of Erasmus, Peter Giles. Conversations over
mutual concerns developed (as one might expect between two
men of a philosophic bent) into more far-reaching speculation. We
can imagine the shape their speculation took, given the economic
negotiations More had just been party to on behalf of "the most
invincible King of England, Henry, the eighth of that name, who is
distinguished by all the accomplishments of a model monarch"
(to quote the tongue-in-cheek ascription that opens *Utopia*).
They might very well have discussed whether the rapacious world
of international politics was the only possibility open to us;
whether the very different societies at that time being discovered
in the "new world" might have something pertinent to say to the
old; whether an ideal republic such as Plato had proclaimed might
really exist on this earth—and if so, what it would actually look
like.[14]

We do not know what More and Giles said to one another in the course of their conversations, but before the English ambassador returned home in the autumn of 1515 he showed Giles a nearly completed draft of what is now the second book of *Utopia*. It is the minute description of an ideal commonwealth located "somewhere" in the new world, as reported to characters named "Thomas More" and "Peter Giles" by a sailor-philosopher-statesman manqué, "Raphael Hythlodaeus." The bizarre name of this narrator, who actually tells us all we ever know about Utopia, reinforces the puzzling ambiguity that More's punning place-name forces us to confront at the outset. For just as the ideally perfect setting for human life is, literally, *ou-topos*, "no place," so our unique source of information about it is an even more blatant contradiction in terms. He is at once "Raphael," being Hebrew for "the healing of God" (and the name of the angel who guides Tobit in his blindness), and "Hythlodaeus," a Greek confection of a surname which, being interpreted, is something like "Expert in Trifles" or "Well-learned in Nonsense." What we have on the level of nomenclature, then, is the blending of a biblical messenger and a Hellenic joker. The macaronic of his name suggests that we are meant both to trust his guidance and to hold back from doing so entirely. It offers us the paradox of the whole of *Utopia* in minature.

Very soon after returning to London with his manuscript, More was approached by King Henry with an offer: a place in the royal service and a quite decent (and by now, with a growing family, much-needed) pension to go along with it. It was, as his good friend Erasmus wrote him, "whether one looked to the profit or the honor . . . not to be despised."[15] But the possibility of standing close to the seat of power threw More into a quandary: to serve or not to serve. Should he guard his private honor, or risk losing it in the service of a king who was by no stretch of the imagination a "model monarch"? Should he continue to dream of better worlds, as he had done abroad in the company of a like-minded (but powerless) friend, or attempt to influence the course of events of the world in which he actually lived?[16]

The result of this dilemma was an expansion of the original manuscript in such a way as to heighten the circumstances of More's own situation late in 1515. What we get, therefore, is *Utopia's* Book I, in which Hythloday grows beyond his former

role as mouthpiece to become a compelling figure of a man
confronted by the same choice that More himself faced in reality—
to serve or not to serve. It is a predicament already familiar to us,
for in Hythloday we stand once again with Plato before the
prospect of Syracuse and with Isaiah "in the year in which King
Uzziah died." We stand, in other words, at an ancient crossroad
and with a familiar predicament. Should the voice crying in the
wilderness (or, in More's case, dreaming up a utopia) venture to
reveal the truth to a sovereign who might very well listen to reason
and bring the "good place" a little bit closer to hand—or should
he learn from the futility of history, and keep himself pure and
unspotted from the world?

This is the question which Book I repeatedly poses to us, as
Hythloday together with the characters "More" and "Giles"
engage in something like a Socratic symposium. The subject of
their talk, which begins in a fortuitous encounter after Mass one
Sunday during "More's" visit to Antwerp, has to do with the
responsibility of a man of Hythloday's wisdom and experience
toward the political world of Europe. Having already suffered
the reality of life at a prince's court, Hythloday is disinclined to
do more than stand on the sidelines and keep himself out of the
fray. He describes an occasion on which he was a guest at the
table of John, Cardinal Morton, the esteemed Lord Chancellor in
whose household the young Thomas More had once served as a
page, and recounts how a lawyer in Morton's entourage took the
opportunity during dinner to congratulate the nation on its swift
dispatch of thieves. Although England was everywhere infested
with felons, the gallows were busy bringing them to justice. How
odd, then, that criminals were nowhere deterred from their
crime.

Hythloday goes on to tell "More" and "Giles" how he entered
this discussion and turned it around, drawing attention away from
the symptoms of social breakdown, such as a rash of theft, to its
actual source. The rapacious self-interest of the idle rich, who
first impoverished the nation with their greed and then sharply
reduced the poor's chances of earning an honest living, had caused
the very conditions which the "authorities" were now preoccupied
with punishing. Hythloday's prime example of ruling class self-
destruction is an abuse that More, as one close to the cloth industry, knew about first-hand: the enclosure of vast tracks of arable

land for sheep grazing, for the short-term profit of the few and the
destruction of the many. It was, in fact, a policy blindly pursued
by the wool monopoly (under royal protection) which threatened
"to turn all human habitations and all cultivated land into a
wilderness." Sheep that formerly were a source of sustenance to
the people have become like ravening wolves, "so greedy and wild
that they devour human beings themselves and devastate and
depopulate fields, houses and towns," thus turning England's
other Eden into a waste place, where to stay alive means one has
to steal. The rich have left the poor no other recourse. Ironically,
and at great cost to the fabric of the nation, they have created the
thieves who rob them.

In Hythloday's recounting of his speech before Morton and his
retinue, we hear more than the voice of the Platonic philosopher
trying to reason the court of the powerful into self-reflection.
There is also the ringing denunciation of the Old Testament
prophets, of an Isaiah speaking to the heartless rich of ancient
Israel about their total disregard for the poor: "Woe to you that
join house to house and lay field to field . . . shall you alone
dwell in the midst of the earth?" (5:8). And just as Isaiah couples
his remonstrance with a call for what the New Testament prophets
will later speak of as *metanoia*, or repentance—

> Wash yourselves, be clean, take away the evil devices
> from my eyes: cease to do perversely. Learn to do well:
> seek judgment, relieve the oppressed, judge for the
> fatherless, defend the widow (1:16-17)

—so Hythloday follows his passionate exposé of abuses with a plea
for positive change: "Cast out these ruinous plagues. Make
laws . . . Restrict this right of rich individuals to buy up everything. . . . Let fewer be brought up in idleness." The solution to
England's social problems is not capital punishment; it is justice.

The point of Hythloday's plea for reform is to catch Cardinal
Morton's ear. For this reason the philosopher woos the tyrant,
the prophet spends his days in the odious presence of those whose
hands are full of blood, and the Christian humanists of the Renaissance (like Erasmus and later More himself) give their time and
learning to princes. Yet at the very point when Hythloday seems
likely to convince his audience, the venal stupidity of the court

once again takes over, distracting everyone with its pettiness and
flattery. Morton rises up from table, dismisses the whole company, and returns with a sigh to the work of his day. His abrupt
departure seems a sign of a return to business as usual, to a world
in which sheep continue to graze through abandoned farming
villages and the gallows are crowded with thieves to be hanged.
For Hythloday, it shows the utter futility of whistling wisdom in
the wind. The "system" always prevails.

Hanging over the entire discussion, which unfolds with great
emotional force in the course of this recollected exchange, is a
single question that brings home to us the real burden of *Utopia*:
"What is to be done with England?" According to "Giles" and
"More" the answer is a firm, if indefinite, "something." Some
influence for good can be exerted, some amelioration of misery
is worth whatever it takes to bring about. Referring repeatedly
to Hythloday's "favorite author," Plato, they marshal every
argument they can find to lure this particular philosopher into
politics. If only he would make the best of Europe's available
majesties. If only he would adopt a strategy of counsel "which
knows its stage, adapts itself to the play in hand, and performs its
role neatly and appropriately." Because what matters after all
(says "More") is the best *possible* performance. "What you cannot turn to good you must make as little bad as you can. For it
is impossible that all should be well unless all men were good, a
situation which I do not expect for a great many years to come!"
Until the eschaton, he might have said.

The voice which "More" assumes here is rational, accommo-
dating, worldly-wise—the voice of one who acknowledges the
inevitability of limitations and is willing to work within them. But
it is precisely this acceptance of the status quo as both necessary
and inevitable that Hythloday cannot abide. Like every good
utopian, he cannot think in terms of anything less than the total
picture which, like Plato's philosopher-king, he must scrape clean
at the outset lest his vision of justice be contaminated and his
design distorted. Hythloday will not adapt himself to the play at
hand, any more than he will accommodate telling the truth to the
capacity of those who may, if only for the moment, listen. For
him, as for all genuine utopians, it is either light or dark, and not a
shadowy mixture of the two; either black or white, rather than a
whole spectrum of gray; either a total reorientation of society, or

nothing at all. There is no "better," or middle, ground. And if
there is to be a best—an ideal commonwealth—it will be one in
which money and private property have both been abolished, and
all things are held in common.

"More" responds by giving all the traditional arguments
against communism, which are at least as old as Aristotle's critique
of Plato. The abolition of private property would destroy the will
to work, lead to riot and bloodshed, and dissolve the necessary
and order-maintaining hierarchies of society that defend against
forces of anarchy. It would be no brave new world in which
money and private property were outlawed; indeed, it would be
utterly unimaginable as a state of affairs.

For Hythloday (and, of course, for the author who stands
behind him), this objection provides the perfect transition to that
description of the island commonwealth of Utopia, which More
had already imagined during his sojourn in the Low Countries in
the company of the real Peter Giles. "Raphael," the angelic guide
and restorer of lost sight, will rest his case on a single radiant
example of social justice. Seeing will be believing. Hythloday's
five years of first-hand experience in Utopia will serve his inter-
locutors (and More's readers) as a vision of the ideal commonwealth—an enacted ideal which will either corroborate or under-
mine his claim for a still more excellent way. Thus, turning from a
gripping portrayal of the political and economic disorder of
England's ravaged garden, we follow More's three characters into
an Antwerp garden to hear Hythloday's account of a "demi-
paradise" intended both to shame and inspire us.

* * *

The effect of our moving from *Utopia's* first to second book is
meant both to surprise and please, as if after stumbling through
the darkened hallways of a house we used to call home, we should
suddenly push open a door and stand there amazed, looking into
a room full of light. This contrast of worlds, and the disorientation that often accompanies a passage between them, is the stock
in trade of what after Thomas More will come to be called utopian
literature. The reader is always put a little bit in the position of
Alice, stepping through the looking glass into a Wonderland of
fresh possibility and unexpected reversals of value. At point of

entry one typically feels alien and defensive, wondering if home is
really as bad as all that. But then, slowly, as one's eyes become
accustomed to the contours of "no place," one begins to feel less
sure about things back there, which no longer have the force of
inevitable reality to them. What we always took for granted as
normal or necessary can even come, in the light of this new environment, to seem not only perverse but ridiculous. And although
utopian fictions are on the whole a rather dour lot (undertaking
as they do the serious business of diagnosis and cure), they are
perhaps most effective when, as in More's Ur-text, they occasionally make us laugh—at our preoccupations and vanities, at the
absurdity that is the reverse side of our sin, at ourselves. Utopia's
looking glass is also a fun-house mirror.

Whether or not we are entering the best of all possible worlds
as we cross over the threshold of Book II, however, is quite
another question. The author insists, as we shall see, on making us
work toward our own notion of the ideal; he gives absolutely
nothing away. But what is clear from the outset is that More is
not offering us a Hesperidean fantasy or a trip to the Isles of the
Blest. Utopia is not literally an "other Eden." And this is clear
not only because of the continued presence of realities such as
crime, slavery, war and death, but because unlike paradise this
island commonwealth is a human construct—the product of
reason, will, and collective effort—rather than a divine gift.

At the beginning of its history, furthermore, there is a founding father, a creator who called up this ideal "no place" virtually
out of nothing. King Utopus, of course, is modelled along the
lines of Plato's paragon: an enlightened individual whose power
enables him to inaugurate his vision of the good *de novo*. And
so almost two millenia before Hythloday's visit, Utopus conquered a "rude and rustic" native population, organized them
(with the help of his soldiers) to cut off their now common
territory from the mainland by digging a protective channel of
water, and then established throughout the island realm fifty-four
identical cities, each one laid out in rough so that future genera-
tions might adorn them with their own hands. Having thus
separated his Utopia from the rest of the world, and therefore
reduced to a minimum the chance of contamination, he set about
building a new social order from scratch and apparently without
any resistance from the populace (for the beneficiaries of utopian

planning are invariably as compliant as they are malleable!).
Utopus worked with merely a few principles of reorganization.
All persons would work; all would hold property in common; all
atheism, as well as every form of religious intolerance, would be
forbidden. These guidelines would be sufficient to bring about "a
perfection of culture and humanity." Having legislated them into
being through what seems to have been his absolute power,
Utopus then does what no actual tyrant has ever been known to
do. He disappears from his own scene, taking with him the office
of monarchy itself. He is, perhaps, the perfect prince.

What remains in his place, two thousand years later, is a
representative democracy, with a kind of House of Commons
comprised of officials elected annually by groups of families in
each of Utopia's cities, as well as a nationwide senate consisting of
governors, one per town, elected to their office for life. Hythloday shows minimal interest in the workings of Utopian government or in the special training that a governor might be expected
to receive for his lifetime of political service. This is because
government in fact does very little and depends almost not at all
on individual contributions. Instead he focuses our attention on
the commonwealth's primary unit, the family household, whose
ordinary existence demonstrates for him the ideal nature of
Utopian life. What he portrays will not be everyone's familial
dream come true, although it might be expected to please More's
contemporaries more than it does his twentieth century readers.
To begin with, the family is a strict patriarchy in which the
eldest male is the head and the rest of the household assumes a
fixed rank in the hierarchy below him. At worship services, for
instance, husbands hear their wives' confessions, and mothers those
of their children; at table, men are served by women and then
both parents by their offspring. The operating principle within
the family, as everywhere else in Utopia, is that "everything has
its proper place and the general welfare is carefully regulated."

Now as I suggested above, this scheme of things would no
doubt be a great deal more congenial to a Tudor audience, with
its assumption of patriarchy and certain codes of behavior. Even
so, we find a real departure from the norms of More's day in the
measures which are taken precisely to limit the power of the
family, to prevent it from becoming a clan, a selfish "us" willing
to exploit "them" for its own well-being. Once again it is a matter

GOSHEN COLLEGE LIBRARY
GOSHEN, INDIANA

of regulation, and one which begins with the permissible size of
the family unit. No more than sixteen adults are allowed in any
one household; "excess" persons are simply transferred to smaller
ones. Children with particular skills not likely to be nurtured in
the home of their birth are placed with other families in whose
company they are more likely to develop their potential. These
are subtle ways to insure that one's primary identification is not
to "blood," but to the whole community. They are designed to
lessen the intensity of familial egotism in order to prevent the
partisan spirit of clan from dividing the commonwealth asunder.
There are no Lancasters and Yorks on this island.

One can see a generalization of identity and commitment in
other aspects of Utopian life. While mothers nurse their own
infants, attendants care for children between the ages of one and
five, who live in communes apart from their parents. Households
gathered together for meals dine in common, in centrally located
halls, where the food is "professionally" prepared. And lest any
family become unduly attached to the house in which they live,
so that it appears to be theirs and theirs alone, each household
routinely changes residence every ten years. What may very well
seem like an agony to us—appalled at the prospect of a lifetime
spent packing and unpacking books, locating a new apartment,
finding the most reliable dry cleaner—does not seem to constitute
a hardship for this nation of light travellers. They are not
burdened with private possessions, and the houses and neighbor-
hoods in which they live are all more or less alike. There is not
much particularity to get attached to; one house, one town, even
one family is as good as another.

One of the major departures from Plato's *Republic*, let alone
from the England described in Book I, is the fact that manual
labor is universal and respectable. Everyone works in agriculture,
as well as in a particular craft that is traditional to their family.
A tiny percentage of folk are exempted from this expectation,
either on account of infirmity or because they have shown such
exceptional gifts for learning, religious leadership, or public
counsel that they are enabled by society to pursue their several
callings fulltime. (This is a privilege that lasts only as long as they
remain faithful and zealous in their special work. Freeloading
does not exist in Utopia.)

As a result, the fact that everyone works means that no one

must work too much—or even, by Tudor standards, very much at all. There is more than enough to go around. This is not only because of full employment and a universal work force, however; it has to do with the freedom of Utopia from the false needs that drive the rich of Europe to impoverish the poor—the expensive addictions and sumptuous array of material goods that people use to establish their identity over against those who have less. The Utopian knows nothing of the consumerism that is so apparent in portraiture of More's own time, where a realistically portrayed human face surmounts a carapace of jewels and silks and laces that have all but lost their resemblance to functional clothing. Instead, as in the example of the householder mentioned by Hythloday, the head of a family has only to go to market and get what is required by those in his charge. He has but to ask in order to receive, and no one goes without.

Like Plato's ideal republicans, there is a rationality to the Utopians' appetite that keeps them quite "naturally" impelled by genuine need rather than distracted and dissipated by false desire. This is not because they are a nation of philosophers, but because they dwell (as the poetic epigraph to the first edition of *Utopia* states) in a "philosophical city" organized to nurture moderation without having either to teach it abstractly or impose it by force. There is nothing in their society that has ever suggested, for instance, that clothes make the man or that you are as remarkable and sophisticated as the gourmet food you eat. While the rest of the world is driven by avarice, greed and pride—yes, especially by pride, "which counts it a personal glory to excel others by superfluous display of possession"—Hythloday's exemplary householder simply takes whatever he and his family genuinely need, and then moves on. The Utopian's interests and values lead him elsewhere.

Where they lead is to the pursuit of pleasure, which constitutes the chief end of life in Utopia. In so apparently austere a social climate, this may at first come as a surprise. Indeed, it even embarasses the usually all-approving Hythloday to have to admit them to be as "leisure-loving" as they are. It seems, at first, an anticipation of a very modern laissez-faire that stands at odds with the careful general regulation that everywhere obtains. The key to understanding the hedonism which apparently flourishes in this philosophical city lies in the fact that the pleasures they pursue are decent and life-enhancing; the pleasure-seekers themselves, *self-*

regulating. What we find, moreover, is a scale of delights that range from good to better to best (by-passing the bad entirely, apparently because it fails to amuse). On the bottom of this scale there are the various joys of the flesh, a list of which includes the following: eating, drinking, itching, rubbing, evacuation and (to use Hythloday's euphemism) "performing the activity generative of children." It may very well seem a bewildering combination of good times that pairs the pleasures of a bowel movement with those of sexual intercourse. But in this case, as in so many others, Utopian reason is the great leveller. Both activities are useful and necessary, but both become absurd if lingered over, or if exacerbated in order to experience them as often as possible. So it is with all the joys of the flesh. To scratch an itch makes sense, but the man who constantly irritates his skin in order to scratch it (Madison Avenue to the contrary notwithstanding) is both grotesque and more than a little bit crazy. Therefore—and here the reader takes a deep breath, either in amazement or in utter incredulity at the claim—"false pleasures" are neither cultivated nor pursued in Utopia.

What does claim the attention of the citizens, and which can even be characterized as the national passion, are the things of the mind: discussion of happiness itself, debates on the nature of pleasure and value, and attempts to integrate the dictates of reason with the Utopian religious principles that fulfill and crown them. Hythloday summarizes the latter as a belief in the immortality of a soul born for bliss and in a judgment after death to reward virtue and punish vice. On these two hang the life of the commonwealth. Their contemplation constitutes Utopia's deepest and most treasured joy—especially for those who have the intellectual capacity to take them the furthest.

But even for the most ordinary person, the whole point of the day is the free time before or after work which is open to what today we might call "cultural pursuits"—times when the mind is stretched and delights in its exercise. Thus we are told that men and women flock to public lectures in the hours just before dawn (in a cross between monks rising for lauds and "Sunrise Semester"), a lecture which they choose from an array of possibilities according to their individual interests. At meal times they gather in common dining halls for the pleasure not only of nourishing food, but of lively conversation. After dinner there is music, or

more talk, or a variety of games designed to stimulate thought
and develop the moral sense. What Hythloday describes, therefore, is a kind of Chautauqua Institution open every day of the
year and without price of admission: good clean fun in the
midst of an earnest and unrelenting "uplift." It offers us a vision
of an entire society that has become as much as possible a university without walls; a nationwide "work-study" program in
which education is not only the national pastime, but the national
sport.

Perhaps this emphasis on learning and moral improvement
represents the true genius of King Utopus's legacy, constantly
underscoring as it does the rationale for communism as the way
to maintain both the happiness and the good of the realm. True
child of the *Republic*, Utopus realized the crucial role of education in forming the kind of citizen who would be able not only to
live in an ideal commonwealth, but secure it for the future. By
separating his population from the mainland, he in effect created
an island schoolroom in which to teach the populace to know true
needs from false; to place the corporate good above private gain;
to consider the values that motivate and maim the outside world
to be unnatural and therefore repellent. He created a world, in
other words, where people were "set up" to be virtuous rather
than reinforced in the stupidity and evil that characterize the
nations we come from.

What Utopia itself seems to represent for Hythloday (and
quite possibly for the inscrutable More standing behind his
character) is a massive attempt to reeducate humanity in the good,
and thereby to restore us as much as possible to our true identity.
Through universal education it is possible to pluck out vices of
long standing. And to this end there is one lesson that lies at the
heart of the Utopian curriculum and which, having been learned
millenia ago, accounts (at least in Hythloday's eyes) for the perfection of the place. One lesson: private property is at the root of
all social evil and must, therefore, be eliminated. Possessions kill;
gold is lethal; Mammon, the prince of this world, must be toppled
from his throne.

But how? We know from Book I (where money, rather than
reason, turns the wheels) how universal and tenacious a tyrant
Mammon is. What we find in Utopia, however, is the way he can
be defeated—not by "abstract philosophy," but by ordinary social

practice instituted by a king who knew what he was doing. Hythloday gives the Utopian solution by way of describing the commonwealth's demystification of gold. Instead of treating it as a precious commodity to be anxiously guarded or even killed for in desperation, the Utopians leave it in the open and unguarded. In fact, they use it to make their "vessels of dishonor": chamber pots, ordinary kitchen ware, chains, the shackles worn by prisoners and slaves (who are taken from the ranks of would-be conquerers, or from those few who refuse to live in Utopia by its rules). More important still, they teach their children to regard their attachment to all that glitters with outright shame, in a way that reminds one of the behavior modification procedures to be developed far more self-consciously in a later utopia such as B.F. Skinner's *Walden Two*. The procedure begins with decking out children in gold and jewels so that they resemble little Tudor royals in the most outlandish of court regalia. Initially the bright colors and shimmer delight them, but gradually, as the children notice that older brothers and sisters do not dress this way, nor do their soberly apparelled parents—as they realize, moreover, that it is only social pariahs who have gold chains hung around their necks—then, quite naturally, they will with alacrity put away childish things. Such children, says Hythloday to "More" and "Giles," are "just like our own, who when they grown up, throw away their marbles, rattles, and dolls." Except, of course, that what they are throwing away is the outward and visible sign of capitalism, and with it (or so we are asked to believe) the incentive to avarice, greed, and the greatest of these, pride.

A choice example of this coming of age is related by Hythloday out of his own experience. One day, he recounts, the Utopians witnessed to their astonishment the arrival of a group of foreign ambassadors to their shores. The men were dressed to the teeth in silks, pearls, and filigreed necklaces in order to dazzle the local population with their splendor. (Given that Book II was written during More's own stint as a foreign ambassador, it is impossible not to see the author engaged in some humorous self-reflection). The strategy of the diplomatic group is, of course, a familiar one, based as it is on the same rule of Mammon that held sway in Tudor England even as it does today. The gentlemen are dressed for success. In Utopia, however, the tried and true strategy of our world backfires most miserably:

To the eyes of all the Utopians, with the exception of
the very few who for good reason had visited foreign
countries, all this gay show appeared disgraceful. They
therefore bowed to the most humbly outfitted members
of the party as to the masters, but took the ambassadors
themselves to be slaves because they were wearing gold
chains, and so passed over them without any deference
whatsoever.

Why, you might have also seen the children who
had themselves discarded gems and pearls, when they
saw them attached to the caps of the ambassadors, poke
and nudge their mothers and say to them:
"Look, mother, what a big booby is still wearing
pearls and jewels as if he were yet a little boy!"
But the mother, also in earnest, would say:
"Hush, son, I think that is one of the ambassadors'
clowns."

The effect of this particular episode is both amusing and in-
structive, as one might expect in a work whose subtitle proclaims
it to be "No Less Beneficial than Entertaining." It does in its own
humorous way dislodge us from the thrall of our assumptions,
enabling us for this brief moment of dislocation to think about
the values we are usually reluctant to examine, such as the proper
place of clothing and the utter zaniness of a status-obsessed
culture which allows fabric and label to "make" the person who
wears them. For a brief instance we readers may also feel ourselves uncomfortably in costume. Perhaps we will consider for the
first time what it might be like to live in a society in which less
psychic energy and personal expense were lavished on the act of
dressing up, and where the distinguishing attributes of a person
were determined by inward qualities or acts of charity rather than
by the possession of needless material goods.
At the end of Hythloday's humorously subversive story, he
mentions that the foreign ambassadors to Utopia were so crest-
fallen after their failure that "for shame they put away all the
finery with which they had made themselves haughtily conspicuous, especially when, after familiar talk with the Utopians, they

had learned their ways and opinions." To know this ideal commonwealth is not only to love it; it is also to want to go and do
likewise, to be conformed to its world. The moral seems to be
that no booby is big enough to resist the good sense of Utopia.
For in the light of reason (and within a social territory which is
illumined by that light), there is the likelihood that even the most
vapid worldlings will come to their senses, realizing at last both
the foolishness of "conspicuous haughtiness" and the unpreten-
tious delights of dressing down. Thus people can, if not be born
again, then at least be reeducated. They can be encouraged for
good as well as for ill.

But if this example of education by social pressure is the
lesson to be learned, there is an aspect of it that must be noted—
and, perhaps, noted with alarm. What I am referring to is the
prominence of *shame* in the ambassadors' decision to put off
their showy clothes; the extent to which we see them shaped by
a consensus rather than converted rationally to a new point of
view.[17] Realizing this, one remembers as well the shame of little
children upon first noticing who was wearing gold chains and who
was not. But these are in no way isolated instances. Throughout
Hythloday's description of Utopia we are reminded time and time
again of the same phenomenon: how families prefer to dine in
common rather than at home because the latter, while certainly
possible, is considered indecent; how divorce is extremely rare
for the single fact that it is so shameful; how people are kind to
cripples and fools because to be otherwise is to bring great dis-
grace upon oneself; how those who break one of King Utopus's
ordinances (such as mandatory belief in the immortality of the
soul) are so dishonored as to be ostracized and treated as sub-
humans, or exiled outright. Depart, we never knew you.

Together with the strong internalization of social norms,
which ordinarily means that for the individual the idea of breaking with the group is too painful to be borne, there is also an
extensive outward surveillance of behavior in Utopia. To prevent
sedition, representatives to the island's senate may not take
private counsel with one another: it is considered a capital
offense for two or three to be gathered together. Dinner conversation is also carefully monitored by the household elders, "who
restrain the younger folk from mischievous freedom in word and
gesture, since nothing can be done or said at table which escapes

the notice of the old present on every side." Geriatric power
maintains the commonwealth's decorum.

For this reason, too, Utopian travel is carefully supervised.
There is nowhere on the island, Hythloday notes with glee, in
which to find "any license to waste time, nowhere any pretext to
evade work, no wine shop, no ale house, no brothel anywhere,
no opportunity for corruption, no lurking hole, no secret meeting
place. On the contrary, being under the eyes of all, people are
bound either to be performing the usual labor or to be enjoying
their leisure in a fashion not without decency"—in a fashion, that is,
of which the Utopian fathers approve. The commonwealth, he
goes on to say, "is like a single family." In other words—and to
speak less positively than Hythloday—it is impossible for any
Utopian to ever really grow up and leave home, to evade the
grandparental watch, to escape the notice (if I may borrow an
Orwellian anachronism) of the collective Big Brother. With the
evils of private property and egocentric autonomy has also gone,
it would seem, the possibility of privacy as well.

And having admitted that, there come to mind a host of other
aspects of life that are also missing from the scene. Is it merely an
oversight on Hythloday's part, for instance, that no one in Utopia
has a name, or that no one makes a distinctive move or a memorable gesture? Is it simply decadence on my part to crave some
touches of distinction or individuality, whether it be in landscape,
neighborhood, routine, or even in clothing? In this society everything has been done to break down the structures of possession,
prominence and pride—and all, one assumes in good faith, for the
greater good of the commonwealth. But what of the ordinary
goods of human existence? Am I really to be allowed no favorite
tie, no enduring attachment to my boyhood home, no variation on
the daily theme of enlightenment-work-enlightenment except a
change in pre-dawn lecturer or in my edifying after-dinner game?
How much ethical culture can a body stand?

Granted, everyone in Utopia eats and drinks and cultivates the
mind, which is no small accomplishment for any society and
perhaps well worth the exchange of many spurious "freedoms."
Granted, as well, that there is no reason to long for whatever flesh-
pots existed before King Utopus's revolution, when the rich had
more than their fill and the poor (as in our world) were sent
hungry away. But with the eating and drinking done decently and

in order, is it also possible to be merry here? To be sure, Hythloday's account of the visiting ambassadors is very funny, but it is
we, the readers of the episode, who laugh. The Utopians themselves only wag their heads in dismay, or (if they are in the know)
in outright disapproval. We waver between the profit and the
loss: a just society, over which the communitarian banderole
waves "From each according to his talents, to each according to
his needs," or an atmosphere in which spark, idiosyncracy,
passion, and excitement have been placed under wraps. Virtue
reigns and (at least for this interloper into Hythloday's paradise)
boredom creeps in. With so many avenues of self-interest blocked,
it seems that there has been a corresponding cancellation of the
individual, an erasure of the personal that has meant, however
admirable the intention, some destruction to the human spirit.
Unlike Plato's *Republic* Utopia has not banned its poets, but it is
difficult to imagine what poetry could ever be written there,
what jokes told, what art produced. The imagination, dangerous-
ly disruptive force that it is, seems too thoroughly domesticated.
    There are also other aspects of Utopian life that need to be
brought to the fore in this spirit of objection: the institution of
slavery, for instance, or the imperialist annexation of other
territories to meet the needs of Utopia's expanded population.
There is also the commonwealth's use of sabotage, assassination,
and mercenary soldiers to wage foreign war, as well as their
avoidance of treaties. Eventually the question we are left with is
the obvious one: is this "little world, this precious stone set in the
silver sea" really the *ideal* commonwealth, the practical demon-
stration of Plato's philosophical city?
    For Raphael Hythloday, Utopia is the uniquely good place on
earth. Its citizens (to quote his final speech to "More" and
"Giles") "have extirpated the roots of ambition and factionalism,
along with all the other vices." Having cast away money, they
have also done away with pride, and in so doing "have laid the
foundations of the commonwealth not only most happily, but
also to last forever, as far as human prescience can forecast." The
right plan is in place, world without end. But having made his
point, to what degree are we meant to share it? How reliable is
this Hythloday, whose last name, let it be remembered, means
"Well-learned in Nonsense"?[18] And why, come to think of it,
did he ever leave the island in the first place? Is there, finally,

something uninhabitable about Utopia that no one could bear it for very long—is it too much of a good thing? Could *nobody* stick it out?

When we turn from these unanswerables (which remain, as we shall see, the stock in trade of utopian critique), and move instead to the ultimate question of what the author himself intended by getting us "nowhere," we realize that Thomas More has made it impossible for us to share his conclusions on any of these matters. He stands mysteriously behind his work, steadfastly refusing to show his own hand, refusing to tell us what to think, but forcing us instead to think for ourselves. His *Utopia* is an invitation to open the door on possibility. And just as "More" confesses to Hythloday in conclusion his wish for "another chance to think about these matters more deeply and to talk them over . . . more fully," so too the work in drawing to its close implicitly asks us to go on talking and thinking, weighing Hythloday's report against our own experience and reactions, using the text, in fact, to discover our own minds. It is in this way a superb piece of dialectic, and one of which Plato himself would be proud.

For what this journey to nowhere gives us is an opportunity for imaginative *Lebensraum*. Located off the map of actuality, and in a sustained way very gently pulling our leg, Utopia nonetheless opens up a breathing space in the midst of our business as usual. In that mental clearing it asks us to rethink the status quo, whether it be that of a fictional commonwealth or our own; to separate truth from fantasy, wheat from chaff. It invites us for a season to discover a new and fictional world in order to return us to our old reality, more conscious and more responsible than before. Confronting the reader with an ideal order—or, at the very least, with an idea of order to try on for size—Utopia offers us the chance to think about how society might be otherwise. It asks us to assess our nature and our institutions radically, and then to make choices on moral, as well as practical, bases. It attempts to prepare us for change.

And it is precisely the element of mutability, so often missed in discussion of More's work, that needs to be underscored in coming closer to *Utopia's* distinctively Christian sensibility—its recognition of human finitude and incompletion. It is here that More's commonwealth makes one of its major departures from its intellectual model. For while Plato readily saw change as befitting

the unreformed world outside the philosopher's construct, he gave
no place to it within. The pattern was divine, and therefore static
and immutable; the republic shall not be moved. By contrast,
Utopia is a society open to new ideas and new life. More particularly, it is open to the in-breaking of that divine will which is
always understood to lie beyond whatever the commonwealth
already knows about it. And so, in prayers that conclude the
"Final Feast"—a religious festival that expresses the furthest reach
of the Utopians' pre-Christian theism—the citizens not only thank
God for their "happiest commonwealth," but also ask to be shown
whatever may be more pleasing to God than they have yet discovered, being "ready to follow in whatever path He may lead."
Because of this openness to further revelation, they are able to
grasp the truth of the gospel when they hear it from the Christians
in Hythloday's party. Because of it, their good but imperfect
commonwealth is willing to be led beyond itself. Their religion
keeps them open to surprise. Unlike the "Christian" states of
Europe glimpsed in Book I, Utopia counts its blessings and prays
for more. At its growing edge, it lives in expectation of God's
lead; it lives, in other words, in hope.[19]

More's work itself, however, seems to leave us in a doubtful
mood. The figure who bears the author's name reflects at the
end of Hythloday's lengthy disquisition, "I readily admit that
there are very many features in the Utopian commonwealth
which it is easier for me to wish for in our countries than to have
any hope of seeing realized." It is characteristic of this enigmatic
little book that "More" does not mention *which* of these features
he admires. None of the burden of analysis will be taken from our
shoulders, nor will we be told what to do with all that we have
been given. But what is most striking to me in these closing lines
of adieu is their melancholy resignation. They form a sad but
realistic exit from an otherwise exuberant fantasy, preparing the
reader to return to a fallen world which, by Christian standards,
has been given so much more than Utopia, and yet which has
done infinitely less to realize peace and good will on earth.

Shortly after Thomas More published his work, he accepted
Henry VIII's request that he assume a position in the Royal
Council. It was the beginning of a state career that would lead
him in a decade's time to the position of Lord Chancellor, and
then within twenty years to the Tower of London and its

chopping block. No doubt during this time he continued to dream
of a more ideal "no place" on earth, even as the prospect seemed
more and more fantastic than it did in 1516. But unlike Raphael
Hythloday, he did the best he could with the England that was at
hand—and kept his future hopes on that New Jerusalem, whose
divine commonwealth was finally the only one worth living or
dying for. One of the most urbane of men, and under no illusions
about human goodness, he most certainly realized that while we
are bound to struggle toward a just social order, no amount of
social engineering or educational enlightenment could eliminate
the war within our members. After all, even after he dressed himself in the splendid robes of state we see in Holbein's famous
portrait, he wore the penitent's hair shirt close to his flesh, beneath
the velvet and ermine. It was a reminder that the philosopher,
too, is a sinner, in need of a deliverance he can never provide for
himself.

Near my home in New Haven there is a Roman Catholic
church which has an inscription above its main entrance that
reads, "Sub Invocatione Beati Thomae Mori." It always strikes me
as ironic that the greatest number of those who have invoked
Thomas More—and invoked not the martyr-saint, but the author
of *Utopia*—are precisely those who would not themselves darken
any church's door, who have used this resolutely inconclusive
work of a Christian humanist as a book to argue their own very
different points of view. Without More's belief in a heavenly city
to keep all notions of earthly perfection in line, all human solutions incomplete, "nowhere" threatens to become each revolutionary's particular "someplace"—a metaphor imposed as reality.
As the course of intellectual history bears witness, More would in
time become a prophet of class struggle to Marx, of the evils of
civilization to Rousseau, of socialism to William Morris, of utili-
tarianism to John Stuart Mill, of British imperialism, bourgeois
democracy, agrarian radicalism. The movements that claim him
seem endless.

All of these varied interpretations of his text testify to the
creative energy that More's fantasy released in the imagination
of the West. During the seventeenth century, it would spawn

other insular realms, while in more recent times, utopia has become global in its extent. But despite all these variations on the theme, we can identify a common legacy in all his offspring, no doubt a larger gift than he ever meant to bestow. By getting us "nowhere," More reminds us that so much of what we accept as our human lot is neither written in stone nor incapable of revision. For what the father of utopia finally asks all his readers to do is take our human powers into more serious consideration. He asks us to realize the enormous extent to which we have doubled our own misery when all the time we had it within our grasp, not only to make things different, but to make them better.

the radiant city

In a letter written to Erasmus just a few weeks before the first appearance of *Utopia*, Thomas More confided a dream to the man who had carried his manuscript to the printer and in every way supported its publication.[20] As usual with so consummate a master of ambiguity as More, it is impossible to say whether the reported dream took place or not. Nonetheless, it provides us with an insight not only into the author's personal fantasy life, but into the classic relationship between a utopian thinker and the desire for political power. What More describes is his own metamorphosis into the figure of King Utopus, crowned with a diadem of wheat, thronged by happy citizens, and welcoming the humanists of Europe to the best of all possible worlds. As long as the dream lasts, he is master of all his imagination surveys. But then the dreamer awakes, and in that return to reality discovers himself to be a philosopher without a kingdom, a merely private citizen whose regal offer of welcome to Utopia turns out to be nothing more than an invitation to a reading. It is all a matter of books in the end.

And a very puzzling book at that, posing problems that are never unravelled and questions that it steadfastly refuses to answer—and not only about the nature of the true commonwealth but about the nature of those who might be expected to live there. In this ultimately disturbing little work, More does not bring the reader back to Eden or to a commonwealth we can ever hope to inhabit. Instead, he leads us to a "nowhere" in which we are able for a time to consider what it is we left behind when humanity was expelled from paradise, to ponder why it is we seem so determined to remain distanced from our own happiness and wretched in a "far country" of our own devising. It asks us why our present life seems so headlessly opposed to the shared well-being we imagine "in the beginning" and which in some form or another might still be possible, even in a sadly fallen world.

But while generous in affording us many treasures of speculation and possibility, *Utopia*'s greatest gift is precisely the one that it finally withholds: the truth and applicability of its message for us. Rather than offering any straight-forward program of reform, it gives us a set of prompters and gets us to do the interpretive work ourselves; it makes us think. Thus, like all metaphor, its goal is to return us to our ordinary reality both disoriented and refreshed. It means to be an eye-opener.

But what if we were meant to take the notion of utopia more literally than More intended? What if a real utopia grew up out of a book written about one, so that instead of being relegated to the region of the fantastic, a portrait of an ideal world-order might actually be looked on as a future possibility? The question I am entertaining here in fact describes the development of utopian thought over the course of the eighteenth and nineteenth centuries, when revolutions, ideologies, and new notions of progress all made it seem as if "nowhere" could find a real place on the world historical map. Although Karl Marx, for instance, was fiercely disdainful of what in the *Communist Manifesto* he called "duodecimo editions of the New Jerusalem," he nonetheless forecast his own version of the "good time" that eventually would have so powerful an impact on both imagination and reality—the vision of a classless society in which the state has withered away and the "higher phase of communism" inaugurated a deliberately *unspecified* condition of human fulfillment. Yet a number of elements link the anti-utopian Marx with the author of *Utopia*. They share an opposition to the antithesis of mental and physical labor, emphasize the all-important distinction between true need and false appetite, and tie the well-being of the individual to that of the society at large. But what is so very different is that More's object of contemplation and dialectical discussion is Marx's call to arms; *Utopia*'s fantasy island is Marx's industrialized Europe transformed by class warfare and the dictatorship of the proletariat. Marx does not want readers of fiction to consider alternatives and come to their own decisions about the true state of a commonwealth; he wants revolutionaries to fight on behalf of that spectre which was even then, in the mid-nineteenth century, "haunting Europe."

In the wake of revolutions that either failed or never occurred, however, what we find is a reawakening of the utopian imagination which, while incorporating many features of Marxist analysis, rejected its violence, its radical challenge to the bourgeoisie and its vehement condemnation of religion. In the spirit of this "Utopia Victoriana" peaceful evolution replaces the upheaval of class warfare, as good times await us beyond the dark horizon of contemporary society like the fair weather that inevitably must follow on the bad. Where Marx and Engels refused to be specific about the classless society, late nineteenth- century novelists such as Edward Bellamy (*Looking Backward*, 1888), Theodore Hertzka (*Freeland*, 1890) and William Morris (*News from Nowhere*, 1891) rushed in to supply optimistic views of a future standing before us, white unto harvest. As Bellamy wrote to the editor of the *Boston Transcript* shortly after his account of Boston in the year 2000 first took America by storm, the sufferings of the present time portend a new and blessed era which is amazingly near at hand. *"Looking Backward* was written in the belief that the Golden Age lies before us and not behind us, and is not far away. Our children surely will see it, and we, too, who are already men and women, if we deserve it by our faith and by our works."[21]

The theological cast of this utopian prohecy comes as no surprise. Bellamy was descended on both sides of his family from a long line of New England clergymen, who joined a concern for public morality to a more personal preoccupation with individual salvation. By 1850, the year of his birth, this austere Calvinist heritage had modified into the gentler Baptist evangelicalism of his father. Where it retained something of its original force was in his mother's Puritan highmindedness, especially as it expressed itself in an abhorrence of selfishness and a belief that personal conversion was the only escape from guilt and estrangement. In his mid-twenties Bellamy would leave his father's church, and with it formal connection to any "established" form of Christianity. But the Protestant spirituality and civic ethos that he learned at home remained powerful influences in his own utopian thought, which is itself a vision of economic and political reform predicated on the experience of mass (even global) conversion. If More's Utopia represents an insular fresh start, Bellamy's presents a world which has been born again.

Too young to fight in the Civil War, and yet profoundly moved by the notions of glory and self-sacrifice it evoked, Bellamy hoped for a career in the military and applied to West

Point. When prevented by poor health from realizing that dream,
he chose instead (like Thomas More) to prepare for a career in
the law, where he anticipated a noble life of service on behalf of
the same wretched poor he had known from childhood in the
dreary mill town of Chicopee Falls. His first case after passing
the Massachusetts bar, however, involved the prosecution of a
woman who had failed to pay her rent. When the judge's verdict
led to her eviction, Bellamy decided that the legal profession was
not for him.

Instead he entered the world of journalism, first in New York
and then in Massachusetts, which gave him a chance to exercise
what was turning out to be his own "prophetic" ministry of
ringing denunciation and calls to reform. Against the complacency of the few who pursued their private interests in total
disregard of the beleaguered welfare of the many—the poor, urban,
immigrant, and often very young—he exposed the corruption of
what had come to be called the "Gilded Age" in a series of articles
whose headlines reveal the range of his social concerns: "Over-
Production and Over-trading," "Overworked Children in Our
Mills," "Riches and Rottenness," "Wastes and Burdens of
Society." Rather than a philosopher like Plato in search of his
educable tyrant, Bellamy was more an Isaiah or a Jeremiah, quite
literally "publishing abroad" his outrage over the inequities of
American life. Like many another intellectual shocked by the
"riches and rottenness" of the post-civil war period, he inveighed
against the breakdown of old moral values, the failures of Reconstruction, and the flood of unchecked entrepreneurial ambition
from which there flowed a vast human misery.

Bellamy could not find in the Christianity he inherited a
viable spiritual counterforce to the various energies of national
self-destruction he saw fomenting disaster and revolution around
him. But having endured what he described as a period of
"profound anxiety and longing almost to sickness" following on
his formal break with his parents' church, he emerged with a
substitute if tentative faith—what in an essay-manifesto of 1874
he was to call a "Religion of Solidarity."[22] In that seminal piece
of writing, he argues that there is within each of us both a "personal" and an "impersonal" drive. The former works within the
realm of the private consciousness, with its selfish appetites and
entirely limited concerns. It is the force that rules the Gilded

Age, with its glaring contrasts of private wealth and mass poverty, indifference and victimization. But there is within us another option—the "not-self"—that can experience what lies beyond individual consciousness: the infinite, the divine, but most importantly for this Religion of Solidarity, the common identity that each of us shares with a universe of other persons.

Bellamy held that we could begin to experience the "not-self" through romantic or familial love or, on a grander and ultimately more worthwhile scale, through submerging oneself into the life of a group, as he imagined possible in the Union Army. He valued, in other words, whatever "takes the form of loyalty or patriotism, philanthropy or sympathy." Instead of calling for a journey to another, more temperate world, however, the Religion of Solidarity asks for a fundamental change in our own. And so, in a bid for an entire society to be born again, Bellamy declares our hope to lie in a national conversion, a change of heart that would lead to a renewal of mind and will, and in that way to a transformation of social reality. In a mix of Emersonian transcendentalism, evangelical piety and an emphasis on education for social change that is at least as old as Plato's *Republic*, Bellamy's new faith is a call to relinquish the ephemeral pleasures of egocentricity for the more profound and lasting good of the common cause. There was no thought, he later confessed, "of contriving a house which practical men ought to live in, but merely of hanging in mid-air, far out of the reach of the sordid and material world of the present, a cloud palace for an ideal humanity."[23] What he ended up producing, however, was a vision of American society on the brink of a new millenium that many people not only wanted to inhabit, but to have some hand in bringing about.

Looking Backward sold sixty thousand copies in its first year and over one hundred thousand in the next. A fifty cent paperback edition put it within easy financial reach, while publication abroad provided an international audience. With so many people hungry for change, the book and its utopian vision proved Bellamy to be an exception to the rule: it made him a prophet with honor in his own country. People found in *Looking Backward* something to read *toward*. But they were also interested in something more active than the turning of pages. In 1888 the first Edward Bellamy Club was organized in Boston for the purposes of discussing the novel and agitating for its principles more effectively. In just two years time the first club was followed by more than one hundred and sixty others, while a Boston-based magazine, *The Nationalist*, attempted to spread the word to the "enlightened" professional class which Bellamy especially wanted to attract. In 1892 the author even turned politician on behalf of the newly formed People's Party, in an attempt to give an enthusiastic group of readers the opportunity to vote for their favorite book. Only four years later the Party collapsed, but by then both Republicans and Democrats had included Populist concerns in their platforms. Bellamy had been vindicated in part by being co-opted. At the end of his life in 1898 he finished a sequel entitled *Equality* (1897), which promised to give an even fuller account of the Golden Age to come.

* * *

Bellamy wrote *Looking Backward* as a fantasy, and then added a touch of mild romance for good measure. It proved to be a successful formula for popular fiction—a seduction into enlightenment—although many readers today may find the Victorian "sugar-coating" unbearably sweet. The book opens with a fictional preface, dated December 26th of the year 2000, which sets up the autobiography to follow: the reflections of Julian West, a nineteenth-century Bostonian catapaulted forward in time by more than one hundred years and now "looking backward." It is a retrospective not only on his own personal experience, but on the collective journey which America has undertaken since 1887, the year he "left" his former age. There is a great deal of backing and forthing throughout the novel, as we are asked to bury a past which is really Bellamy's present—the dreary ways of unbridled capitalism—and anticipate a halcyon future of "National Socialism," which is supposedly the way things already are in the year 2000! The effect of all this will be to make us feel that the world of the 1880's is hopelessly out of date and behind the times. And because in Bellamy's work the distance we travel is calculated in time rather than space, it comes as no surprise that Julian West's birthplace, Boston, remains the stable hub of this universe of change, our point of comparison between then and now. In order to assess the full drama of change, the place where this transformation is to be experienced is constant—the most venerable of

American cities, seen both "before" and "after." In Bellamy's
pages, utopia has come to our town.

The novel's plot is both simple and contrived. Julian West,
as he describes himself during his last fateful day in the nineteenth century, is meant to represent a character type which a
mass audience would at once envy and despise: a Boston Brahmin
who has never known a day's work in his life. For him the turmoil
of labor disputes and worker misery means only that his luxurious
new house is still under construction. It is to be a suitable villa
in a good neighborhood, fit to receive the bride he plans to install
once the feckless builders get back to work and thereby allow him
to get on with his happy life. What will that life actually consist
of? A society marriage, the selection of expensive furnishings for
an elaborate private household, a full round of dinner parties and
musicales, a future spent clipping coupons and watching an
inherited fortune steadily grow. It seems a carefree enough existence to look forward to, except that it is menaced on all sides by
a sea of angry workers so stirred up by their own deprivation (and
the agitation of anarchists) as to threaten not only West's privi-
leged lifestyle, but the fabric of society itself. His spendid house
may be finished only to be swallowed up by chaos; he may live
to see it in ruins.

It is thoughts like these, perhaps overlaying an uneasy con-
science, that plague Julian West at night and keep him from sleep.
To get away from the turmoil of the city he builds a soundproof
chamber below the cellar of his old home, a subterranean retreat
to which "no murmur from the upper world ever penetrated."
Yet it too fails to protect him from the events brooding above
ground, and here Bellamy's point is hard to miss: it is impossible
even for the rich to bury their heads in the sand or to keep reality
at bay. And so West engages a hypnotist to induce a trancelike
state so deep that it can only be broken by his valet, who is the
only other person to know about the underground room. But on
the night of May 30, 1887, in the course of a fire that burned the
house to its foundations, the servant dies in the flames and West
is left below in a state of suspended animation—left, that is, until
a future time when excavations around the property discover the
subterranean chamber and Julian still asleep within it. The person
who breaks the trance is a Dr. Leete, who welcomes Julian to a
September day in the year 2000.

Bellamy's tactic is to join Sleeping Beauty to Rip Van Winkle, and envelop them both in a nineteenth-century fascination with altered states. This aspect of the book was no doubt a great deal of its selling point, but beyond the ploy to catch a reader's attention there is a deeper mythic pattern as well. For what Bellamy does in the contrived burial and resuscitation of Julian West is use the experience of one representative man to figure the death and resurrection of the entire social order of the American nineteenth century—of the "West," in fact. In this character's blinking eyes and mental disorientation upon waking we are to see the Gilded Age itself, stumbling out of its own tarnished sleep as it steps into the purer light of a new utopian day.

Julian's first glimpse of this brave new world overwhelms him. In a heartstopping moment of future shock, as he is taken by Dr. Leete to the bellevedere of his house, he sees the city of Boston—his home town—utterly transfigured. It is a vista which reveals no remembered landmarks, not even the familiar gold dome of the State House that one should have thought to be, if not eternal, then at least able to weather life until the twenty-first century. But this American utopia has cut its losses with the past, even as More's King Utopus separated his commonwealth from all contact with the mainland. Behold, all things are made new:

> At my feet lay a great city. Miles of broad streets,
> shaded by trees and lined with fine buildings, for the
> most part not in continuous blocks but set in larger or
> smaller enclosures, stretched in every direction. Every
> quarter contained large open squares filled with trees,
> along which statues glistened and fountains flashed in
> the late-afternoon sun. Public buildings of a colossal
> size and architectural grandeur raised their stately piles
> on every side. Surely I had never seen this city nor
> one comparable to it before.

Geography remains the same, but everything human in this city-scape has been born again. Viewing the scene through Julian West's eyes, it is impossible not to think of St. John the Divine in the face of his vision of the New Jerusalem—had he, like Bellamy, enjoyed access to the ideal city plans of the Renaissance, or the

gardens of Versailles, or the fantastically idealized urban land-
scapes of an American painter like Erastus Field, whose canvas,
"Historical Monument of the American Republic," presents its
panorama of "stately piles on every side." It is nothing less than
a view from Mt. Pisgah into the Promised Land.

Keeping all these associations in mind, it is important to
remember that what Julian West sees is the same city in which he
grew up and from whose grim reality he has suddenly been
awakened. It is not the eschatological Jerusalem awaiting us at
the end of time, but *Boston*—a happy transformation of that
strife-torn city of 1887 where Julian could not get his house built
or enjoy a peaceful night's sleep. In other words, we see a beautiful butterfly that has lost all resemblance to the larva it once was.
Yet there is still an organic relationship between these two stages
of development that is crucial to our understanding of the change.
This point is driven home by Dr. Leete during his initial conversations with West—conversations which, I regret to say, have all the
charm and spontaneity of a freshman orientation lecture. If the
utopian society of the year 2000 presents a radical departure from
nineteenth-century America, it is a departure that moves along a
single historical trajectory. *This* Boston is the adult stage of what
was in West's century a terrible adolescence. Not only does utopia
constitute an evolutionary leap forward, it also represents the
maturation of humanity. Utopia is the world come of age.

How West's society grew up into the one to which Dr. Leete
introduces him reads like a strange amalgam of economic determinism and the Social Gospel: a Sunday School rewrite of Karl
Marx. As the nineteenth century continued on its ruinous course,
with wealth being consolidated into fewer and fewer hands, it
remained for the twentieth century to discover the one grip large
enough to hold it all together. Rather than some unimaginably
wealthy robber baron or captain of industry, however, the capitalist to end all capitalists turned out to be the nation itself, organized as a business corporation. Bellamy's dream is that of every
socialist, but (as always in utopia) carried to an extremity. There
has been a total transformation of private wealth into the collective hands of the people. We might expect that so radical a social
readjustment would entail violent revolution, but the process
followed an altogether different course from the one predicted by
Marx and Engels. There was an *evolution* of the peaceable

kingdom. America stepped forward into the millenium without
ever having to go through tribulation or apocalypse. It achieved
utopia without tears.

This transition from heartless capitalism to a benign "national
socialism" is presented as the inexorable outcome of economic
forces. Utopia was the necessary outcome of history; it had to
happen. But the reason it happened without the shedding of
blood has to do with a change of heart and a renewal of mind—
in short, an experience of conversion. And it is precisely here, in
the realm of the heart and mind, that Bellamy places his emphasis,
no doubt because this is the realm where his own power as a
utopian writer lay. A small group of enlightened souls—spiritual
"advance men"—were able to see beyond the conflict of class
interests to the national solidarity that formed an almost mystical
bond between all. Thus utopia begins in Bellamy's mind not with
a single philosopher-king, but with a group of visionaries and social
prophets whose purpose turns out to be identical to his own in
writing *Looking Backward*—the celebration of the nation "as a
family, a vital union, a common life, a mighty heaven-touching
tree whose leaves are its people, fed from its veins, and feeding it
in turn."

According to this myth of history, the future came knocking
on America's door and the entire population was eager to open it
wide. This occurred not because the people knuckled under to
the iron law of economic determinism, but because they had been
truly converted by the eloquent good sense of utopia. Like Julian
West called forth from the tomb of the past, they were born again
into the higher consciousness of the new age. In doing so, they
came to the realization that undergirds this utopia and which in-
forms its every part: the belief that to separate from the "impersonal" life of the many is to uproot oneself from humanity, while
to merge with others is nothing less than divine.

Bellamy's personal model for this common bonding was the
Union Army—or rather his civilian, post-war fantasy of it. In
contrast to the pushing and shoving of private life, where the
motive of personal profit at the expense of others thrust a few
lucky ones forward while the vast majority were trampled under
foot, the hierarchy of the military represented reason and order
and common purpose—the classic *desiderata* of utopia. Bellamy
longed for this "model of intelligent cooperation," this "perfect

concert in action," this "tremendous engine" whose massive
power was scientifically coordinated under a single leadership.
And so, when he set about to imagine how politics and economy
might best merge in his utopian future, he envisioned what
amounts to a peacetime "fighting machine." The entire nation
would be joined together into what he called an Industrial Army,
a militia of production whose citizen-workers would give themselves unstintingly to one another in time of peace as soldiers do
in the midst of war. Everyone would work together for America's
well being.

This vision of a nation at labor is familiar to us from More's
Utopia. But what a world of difference separates that sixteenth
century fantasy, with its nostalgic looking backward from the
Renaissance to an essentially medieval way of life, and Bellamy's
industrial futurism. For while we imagine Hythloday's Utopians
spending their six-hour workdays in cozy family workshops or
weaving by the hearthside—engaged in a household economy of
busy hands involved in cottage industries passed down from
family to family—America in the year 2000 is organized on so
monumental a scale that it utterly dwarfs their handicrafts and
agriculture with its massive factories and assembly lines. Each
author, of course, "perfects" a version of the economy from
which he comes, inclining it toward the past or future depending
on his predilection. And so Bellamy gives us a leap forward from
the industrialization of his own day, to imagine what the machinery of production might produce if it were completely "milita-
rized"—a monument to planning and efficiency beyond the
dreams of any Renaissance idealist of order.

This is not to say that Bellamy intends his Boston to be a
mechanized anthill. It is, rather, that he imagines a degree of
technological development so total that it overwhelms us with
the inhuman scale of its standardized perfection. It is the Crystal
Palace with a vengeance—a massive labor-saving device guaranteed
to keep humanity from earning a living by the sweat of its brow.
For Bellamy the "impersonal" is always the goal, and so he
delights in the prospect of a socially-industrialized mechanism
perpetually in motion, with regiments of gears and valves, pistons
and engines, all happily waging the war of production against the
only enemies left to fight in the twenty-first century: hunger, cold,
nakedness, the legitimate needs of the flesh.

Everyone in this mechanized utopia belongs to the Industrial
Army, although not all are members of its work force. Those on
active duty consist of every male and female between the ages of
twenty-one and forty-five; that is, from the time of life when one
completes formal education until the happy day of retirement.
From that moment on, one is released (as Dr. Leete says) "to
ease and agreeable relaxation." In less than twenty-five years of
active service, therefore, a citizen has earned an entire lifetime's
keep. Jobs are assigned according to individual talents and prefer-
ences after a three year stint of service—a kind of industrial
novitiate. During this basic training, raw recruits are given
society's dirty work to do; once this period is completed, each is
free to select "the harness which sets most lightly on himself . . .
that in which he can pull best." Dr. Leete's metaphor reflects the
real attitude toward work which pervades Bellamy's utopia, with
its harnessed worker and utterly extrinsic personal rewards.
Despite short hours, frequent vacations, and credit card access to
all material needs, even the happiest worker seems inevitably a
cog in the machine. We search in vain throughout *Looking Backward*, as in More's *Utopia*, for any sense of on-the-job interest,
let alone excitement. It is not surprising that no one ever com-
plains about forced retirement at the age of forty-five.

Instead, the pleasure of work lies not in the act of labor
itself—from which everyone is happy to be released—but in the
esteem one garners in the course of duty. Once again, as in
Utopia, we are introduced to a society that is driven by a sense
of honor and, conversely, by the fear of shame. It is a meritocracy
where incentives to excellence have nothing to do with money.
Instead workers seek promotion, badges of merit, and a small
array of honorific privileges simply because they long to progress
onward and upward in the eyes of others. They are consumers
of praise. And yet it must be noted that for those who advance
to the highest ranks of service, their achievement does not come
in response to any vulgar craving for applause. It arises instead
from a deep-seated identification with the "interests of the
common weal." These become the directors of the Industrial
Army and the virtual directors of the nation itself, as the spiritual
descendents of the earliest apostles of nationalism who have
merged their individual selves with the "impersonal" good of all.
Despite the honors that distinguish them, they fit in perfectly

with the multitude, like good soldiers on parade. They are so
good, in fact, that they all but disappear.

And where such paragons go after retirement is the federal
government—or at least what remains of the federal government
once the armed forces, the revenue service, and the treasury have
all been eliminated outright, while the various manifestations of
the justice system (such as judges, jailors, police, and the like)
are cut back to the barest postlapsarian minimum. Each year a
congress is convened so that its members can assist the president,
who is also commander and chief of the Industrial Army, in his
guidance of the national economy. These positions are all filled
by those who are no longer active members of the work force.
It is they who govern what amounts to a geriarchy—a rule by the
elderly that once again finds its complement in More's *Utopia*.
Bellamy thought that those in the thick of production and the
race for honor could not be trusted to have the requisite impar-
tiality it would take to think of the whole nation as one's ultimate
priority. The active work force, therefore, is disenfranchised.
Thus, for all its talk of brotherhood and solidarity, *Looking Backward* remains deeply distrustful of the masses. Utopia is kept
humming by patriarchs no longer in the fray, men who have so
given themselves to the nation it might be said that in their hands
the nation governed itself. It would seem that according to
Bellamy, a collective of philosopher-retirees, well out of the
factory's hubbub, best knows how to keep society on the single
course it has no reason to change.

It is precisely the smoothness and imperturbability of twenty-
first century life that most impresses Julian West, in those previous few moments when he is allowed to escape Dr. Leete's
relentless instruction and follow his daughter Edith around the
Boston of Tomorrow. What he experiences in his trips down-
town—and every reader fervently wishes there were more of
them—is a life made not only easier, but made morally better
through technology. Liberated from the conditions of inequity
that for millenia have made people either ruthless oppressors or
sour victims, humanity is able at last to stand tall. In the words
of a contemporary U.S. Army jingle that Bellamy would no doubt
be the first to hum, it is on the brink of the twenty-first century
that we are free "to be all that we can be." As Julian West strolls
along the streets of this latter day Boston, the crowds he passes

are a far cry from the stooped, resentful mob of 1887, "faces
unmarred by arrogance or servility, by envy or greed, by anxious
care or feverish ambition, and stately forms of men and women
who had never known the fear of a fellow man or depended on
his favor."

"Stately" folk such as these—defined, please note, by all that
they are *not*—choose to live in modest private homes while saving
opulence for public buildings "ornate and luxurious beyond anything the world ever knew before." In contrast to More's Utopia,
with its abolition of private property and simple peasant austerity,
Bellamy's ideal world has no taste for material self-denial. We are
a far cry from the monastic ideal that seems to underlay utopian
schemes in the sixteenth and seventeenth centuries, although
what remains is a commitment to the community at large rather
than to party or self. Gone, however, is the disdain for worldly
goods that kept the Utopians in homespun.

Busy consumers, Bellamy's utopians conserve their time and
energy by shopping in national showrooms, where samples of
every conceivable manufactured good are on display, and are
then whisked home by pneumatic tube. Everyone shops by
credit card ("money" is a dim historical memory) and only to the
limit of their equal resources, which in every case is more than
sufficient. The individuality of the consumer is respected to the
degree that each person may allocate his or her resources differ-
ently. Some, like Edith Leete, favor clothes; others invest a
greater percentage of their income in larger homes or fancier food.
Personality, therefore, is expressed in consumption, and to a
certain extent you are what you buy (a "well-dressed" woman,
a "gourmet"). But as always in utopian schemes, reason prevails.
All things are done, all purchases are made, decently and in order.
Nor are there either anorexics or overeaters, compulsive shoppers
or binge buyers, in Bellamy's golden age. Sufficient means breeds
a regularity of life, an instinct for proportionate behavior and
personal temperance.

In their leisure time, Bellamy's Bostonians take special pleasure in the arts. In picture galleries, for instance, they are amused
by a nineteenth-century painting of a rainy day—a painting in
which they see a crowd of people, each one huddling under a
private umbrella and fighting a private war against the elements,
rather than walking under the sidewalk awnings which now

provide corporate shelter in rain and snow. They assume the
picture to be a satire on the painter's times, an era of selfishness
which they contemplate with a mixture of fascination, amuse-
ment and contempt—like the ideal visitor to a Soviet "Museum of
Superstition," confronted by the barbarous abuses of the past.
The Bostonians also delight in contemporary works of fiction
such as the novel by Berrian, *Penthesilia*, which keeps Julian West
awake all night in astonishment. Plato banished the poets from
his *Republic* because they told lies and were subversive of the
state; in Bellamy's twenty-first century, however, they are much
beloved precisely because they celebrate the new age on its
own rational terms. As Julian opens this book it seems as if we
are going to get a peek at Bellamy's golden age from the inside,
to see how the renewed mind really works and what it is like to
have no need to rob a bank or make a socially advantageous
marriage or unfurl a private umbrella. Imagine, we are asked, "the
construction of a romance from which should be excluded all
effects drawn from the contrasts of wealth and poverty, education
and ignorance, coarseness and refinement, high and low, all
motives drawn from social pride and ambition, the desire of being
richer or the fear of being poorer, together with sordid anxieties of
any sort for oneself or others." It is no wonder West finds his
once-beloved Dickens no longer readable. Social reality has
changed, and so therefore the books people love to read. And yet
in the fictional world which we are asked to consider—a world
without conflict or pain—there would seem to be the possibility
of neither tragedy nor comedy, romance nor mystery. We find
ourselves asking the question of what could actually happen in
Penthesilia.[24]

Instead of going to concert halls, with their limited program
selections available only at fixed times, Bellamy's music lovers
of the future prefer to listen to "radio" performances over the
telephone. They enjoy acoustically superb listening rooms or
bedside receivers—technical fantasies that we have come to know
as twenty-four hour broadcasting and elevator Muzak. West
learns to his delight that whatever he wants is available at any
hour of the day or night, and to a degree of professional perfection that has rendered "live" music, let alone amateur music-
making, utterly obsolete.

In this same music room, it is possible of a Sunday to choose

among an assortment of sermons. And so, at the appointed hour,
Edith Leete summons Julian West to the listening apparatus to
hear what is for him, at least initially, the eerily disembodied
voice of a radio minister, a Mr. Barton. He preaches only by
telephone, and to an audience often reaching 150,000. What
West hears over the air waves is a theological reprise of everything he has learned and experienced thus far. Barton bemoans
the dark days of the past and gauges how far the moral revolution of the twentieth century has carried America. He orients us
to that "fraternal standpoint" which is both the secret of human
progress and the substance of his gospel—the *kerygma* of Bellamy's
utopia. For in coming to think of ourselves not as isolated beings,
but as members of a mystical body of national proportion, we
have rolled the stone away from our own tomb. We have raised
ourselves up from the ground and out of a living death. And all
of this in the course of a century: an America that seems "nothing
less than paradise"! No wonder the average person assumes that
the promised millenium is already at hand.

In a breath-taking claim that stands out even in so breathless a
"song of ourselves" as this sermon, Barton says, "For the first
time in human history, mankind is tempted to fall in love with
itself." And yet his real goal is not to plunge us into the depths
of self-congratulation; like Bellamy, he is still too much the son of
Puritan preachers to rest easy in Zion for long. And so, as the
sermon draws to a close, he begins to press us forward to a calling
still higher, like a latter day Pico reminding us that our development is "limitless." For even in the year 2000, America is still
growing toward the eschaton, leaving us even more room for
improvement. On this note the preacher concludes his peroration,
taking leave of his 150,000 listeners in an incandescent burst of
rhetoric:

> With a tear for the dark past, turn we then to the
> dazzling future, and, veiling our eyes, press forward.
> The long and weary winter of the race is ended. Its
> summer has begun. Humanity has burst its chrysalis.
> The heavens are before it.

What Bellamy offers us is something more than "inspiration,"
although its peculiar kind of religious enthusiasm no doubt

accounts in part for the tremendous success of *Looking Backward*, which we know occasioned many a real Sunday sermon after the book's appearance. He presents us with the theological under-pinnings of this utopian vision—and perhaps not of this one alone. For what we find here, as we did in Pico's oration and in Hythlo-day's report of Utopia, is an extravagantly optimistic appraisal of our potential to help ourselves, given the right attitudes and conditions. Human nature is intrinsically good and without limit in what it can both do and be; "sin" is a matter of environmental conditioning and (like crime in the year 2000) can largely be eliminated. In the words of Mr. Barton's credo, "We believe the race for the first time to have entered on the realization of God's ideal of it, and each generation must now be a step upward."

When Julian West comes to himself after hearing this sermon, he feels depressed, full of remorse for having been so ignorant a sinner back in the dark mean days of the nineteenth century. But perhaps the reader is less persuaded that what we have experi-enced of America in its apparently millennial state is indeed the realization of God's ideal. Aside from the smugness that seems an environmental hazard of every utopia, there seems to me in this particular commonwealth a disparity between what we are told and what we observe with our own eyes. For in the midst of so many protestations of solidarity, the "fraternal standpoint," the "cohesive force of society," and so on, we see almost no signs of actual social interaction. Crowds flow into the magnificent eating halls like a great human sea, but then disappear into separate dining rooms. Shopping has no social component to it, being a mere transaction of order blanks processed by a clerk. Nor does one attend a concert with other people, or even go to church in order to worship in community. No doubt the invention of telephone-televisions will eliminate attendance at theatres. Iron-ically, then, technological advance seems to have enabled folk to be alone to a degree unknown in the nineteenth century. With "solidarity" there has also come the possibility of isolation.

There is also a pervasive blandness to the population, at least as we see it in the Leetes. They are rational, polite, noble in spirit, unfailingly considerate of the extraordinary stranger in their midst. But without a past to speak of, or any appreciable varia-tion in temperament, or that sense of life's ambiguities that make us both real and amusing to one another, they are exactly the sort

of people who would be unbearable in large doses. They resemble
the monumentally antiseptic city in which they live, having no
particularity of their own, no hidden corner reserved for either
spontaneity or surprise. With "Of course" and "Of course not"
as their range of response, they embody the flattened affect that
Bellamy's vision of the "impersonal" life would seem to require.
Long before he had written in his notebooks about the improved
humanity of the future: "We look for a placid race that shall not
alternate between honey and vinegar, but live on mild ambrosia
ever."[25] In *Looking Backward* he begins to make good on that
promise.

What I am perceiving as an absence of spirit in these citizens
of the twenty-first century may simply be an indictment of
Bellamy as a writer of fiction, but I suspect my objection has
more to do with utopian imagination in general. It seems to be
an activity of mind which, like the literature it has produced, is
invariably long on theory and short on what the great nineteenth-
century novelists of England, France, and Russia have accustomed
us to think of as "character"—persons who are as mysterious
and nuanced as we are. In utopia, ideas are supreme. It sacrifices
the dangerous possibility for the known thing and upholds the
principles of right order above the messy particularities of human
existence. The price exacted for peace on earth so often seems to
be the dreary decorum utopia portrays.

To be sure, it is no easy accomplishment to present an image
of the happy life. While misery loves company, happiness is a
perverse affair that seems always to escape generalization and the
master plan—to escape, in other words, the strategies of utopian
imagining. The impulse of someone like Bellamy is to find the one
size that will fit all, the "impersonal" solution, the vision of a fulfilled humanity that is utopia's prophecy. And so, like his novelist
Berrian, he attempts to limn a world in which no one shouts, no
one shoves, and no one gets hurt. Bellamy's problem as a prophet
of the new age, however, is that his jeremiad against the nineteenth century is so much more convincing than his portrayal of
happiness in the twenty-first. He asks us to take up residence in a
vision only the "impersonal" among us could ever endure; to walk
on a marble floor, as Emerson put it, where nothing will grow. At
any rate, it is surely an alarming sign that when we accompany
Julian West on his nightmare reentry into the Boston he left

behind—Washington Street "like a lane in Bedlam," chock-a-block
with commerce and noise and "the horrible babel of shameless
self-assertion"—we find ourselves longing to stay, choosing to fight
our way through a bad world that nonetheless pulsates with
energy and uncharted human possibility. Compared to the
shadowless light of utopia, Boston never looked so good!

There is also a specific aspect of Bellamy's America in the
year 2000 that is peculiar to *Looking Backward*, which takes us
out of the realm of the tedious and into that of the foreboding.
For at the root of Bellamy's plan to reshape society, and at the
heart of his prophetic vision, there stands the Industrial Army—
and with it, the military ideal of total obedience to command.
We begin, reasonably enough, with utopia's expectation that
everyone work and find some fulfillment in this act of national
service. But for those who are not so inclined, who violate the
integrity of this society by choosing to opt out of it, there awaits
the harshest punishment this utopia knows: bread, water, and
solitary confinement. Less grievous offenders—"men who have
failed to acquit themselves creditably in the work of life"—are
simply made celibates by the fact that no woman will marry them.
Such treatment is, I suppose, the equivalent of a dishonorable
discharge from the U.S. military. But in the year 2000, there is no
civilian world into which one can vanish anonymously, if in dis-
grace; the Army *is* America. Nor would one find refuge in another
country, for in the evolutionary progress that America has both
realized and spearheaded—as one might well expect of Yankee
entrepreneurs—"national socialism" has become an international
phenomenon. With almost any country's credit card on the way
to be accepted by every other, the world is moving toward one
united state.

The happy effect of this is the end of war between countries,
who share their plenty where once they exchanged their aggres-
sion and greed. But for the outcast who attempts to avoid con-
scription, or who simply wants to live some other way, there is no
place to hide, no place to run. As Dr. Leete tells Julian West,
"Our entire social order is so wholly based upon the Industrial
Army that if it were conceivable that a man could escape it, he
would be left with no possible way to provide for his existence.
He would have excluded himself from the world, cut himself off
from his kind, in a word, committed suicide."

What we hear in these words is the frightening aspect of
utopian imagination, the totalitarian urge that hides within the
impulse toward perfection. For there is always one overriding
idea that must be enforced, a single way out of the human predicament, whether it be *Utopia*'s communism or Bellamy's Industrial
Army. Even when we readers of utopian fiction happily go along
for the ride, we notice that there is something essential missing.
However contentedly the factories hum with consumer plenty
and self-transcendence, it is simply too quiet, too univocal to
support human life as we know it. Nowhere are there the odd
nooks and crannies we have always required, nowhere the alternatives in life style to suit our differences nor the opportunity for
writing cranky letters to the editor about complacency on the
assembly line.

This game can be played according to only one set of rules,
and while it may be true that those rules exist for the very best of
reasons, someone who refuses to play by them—or who wants to
invent another game altogether—is going to be rejected like a virus
repelled by a body in good health. Thus, people in Bellamy's
factories who refuse to work are bearers of an infection that must
be isolated lest they introduce their disease into an otherwise
sterile environment. They cannot be allowed to do damage to
others; they are not allowed to be poor or lazy. The very desire
to be different is, in the end, a kind of suicide.

Every utopia presents itself as the truth about reality and then
creates a world where that consensus prevails absolutely. But
when the impulse to remake society over into one's own image
passes from the sphere of the imagination into the arena of concrete political realization—once "nowhere" sets about to make it
all happen "someplace" in particular—utopia ceases to be a
possible dream and to become instead an awful nightmare. At
least such is the stuff of which twentieth-century counter-
prophecies are made.

no exit

One of the most striking examples of utopian imagination in our time comes not from a statesman like More or a journalist like Bellamy, but from the pen of an architect, Charles Edouard Jenneret, better known as Le Corbusier. Born in 1887—the same year Bellamy's Julian West catapulted out of the nineteenth century and into the twenty-first—Le Corbusier's whole career can be seen as an attempt to give authentic expression to the realities of Machine Age civilization. Looking forward to a golden age that seemed close at hand, which in the late twenties he hoped to see rising from the rubble of the Great War, he envisioned a "world of tomorrow" (as the 1939 World's Fair would popularize it), an image already familiar to us from the New Jerusalem of St. John the Divine to Bellamy's alabaster Boston. Le Corbusier saw the future as an urban dream come true, as a luminously "Radiant City."

In a series of studies first undertaken in 1931 at the request of the Soviet Government and collected three years later under the title, *La Ville Radieuse*, he assumed the prerogative of a utopian thinker to recreate the world according to his own idea of perfection.[26] Grateful to the Soviet government's "reign of intelligence" for asking his advice about the future of their capital, he nonetheless allowed his thoughts about Moscow to encompass the urban *world* of his own time. What was first to be published as *A Reply to Moscow* became a manifesto for the entire twentieth century.

Like other utopian thinkers, Le Corbusier begins with a sense of revulsion. In his case, it is the Western capitalist city itself—and Paris, in particular. Desperately sick, the city's corruption is apparent in every rotting house and sunless courtyard; in the tubercular tenements of the poor as well as in the gimcrack parlors of the bourgeoisie, who use their money to choke themselves with "this flood of totally sterile, innumerable, unlimited proliferating

pieces of nonsense." The city of the early Machine Age has
become a Moloch imprisoning the body of its citizens in "din,
smells, noise, a bubbling poison brew," then going on to destroy
them. "There is no freedom for men in this present age," he
writes, "only slavery. A slavery to which they themselves consent,
and which is no longer even confined within set limits. To live, to
laugh, to be master in one's own home, to open one's eyes to the
light of day, to the light of the sun, to look out on green leaves
and blue sky. No! Nothing of all that for the man who lives in a
city. The man in a city is a lump of coal in a brazier; he is being
burned up for the energy he produces. Then he fades and crum-
bles away."

Le Corbusier enters this scene like a liberator, a self-professed
champion of the freedom of the individual whose task as architect
and city-planner has less to do with bricks and mortar than with
the spirit. His goal is nothing less than "to satisfy men's hearts."
Like Bellamy he will not waste his time with some imaginary
cloud palace or turn away from the practical necessities of life
through some escape into nostalgia. On the contrary, he will
embrace the future, harnessing technology for human benefit and
thereby allowing "evolution" to run its course. The modern
industrial city itself, now the furnace in which we are consumed
like so many lumps of coal, will become the very means of our
liberation. To effect this change no mere readjustment of the
status quo, no partial cure, will do; as always with utopians, the
solution must be total. What is needed is a massive act of demoli-
ton and rebuilding: the construction of a "machine for living"
which, like each of its citizens, will stand tall and free in the open
air. It must be a Promethean act of ingenuity, and one that
Le Corbusier has no hesitation to speak about in the most heroic
of terms: "the great adventure that lies before mankind . . . the
building of a whole new world."

Nor is this notion of global renewal any longer merely a pipe
dream, a utopian fantasy. No, technology has brought the ideal
environment within our reach. Having mobilized on behalf of
death in the Great War, there is no reason why humanity cannot
bring the same intelligence, know-how and machinery to the
service of the living. Le Corbusier's *Radiant City* in fact pulsates
with this sense of possibility, as if the world it addresses stood on
the brink of an evolutionary leap forward. In its pages there is no

doubt that the hour is at hand, the moment history has been
waiting for. There are, even now, working drawings of planned
cities already available, "pieces of paper on which *human happiness already exists*, expressed in terms of numbers, of mathe-
matics, of properly calculated designs." All that stands between
us and the realization of this happy design for living is our own
limitation—the failure of our vision and the calibre of leaders
sufficiently courageous and forward-looking to lead us into the
Golden Age. Even at the moment of his writing there are minds
capable of thinking big and thinking new, minds that have already
torn themselves away from the squalid clutter of the past. "Our
minds," he proclaims in conclusion, "are insisting on a clean
table-cloth."

It is impossible to read these words without realizing Le
Corbusier's close proximity to utopian tradition. It would seem
that the existing world is always too dirty for its antiseptic imagination, too haphazard, too weighed down by the institutionalized
mistakes of the paste. And so Le Corbusier insists on a "clean
tablecloth," a new beginning—even if much of Paris ("racked with
disease . . . becoming impotent and senile on all sides") must be
torn down, its corpse hauled away, in order for the Radiant City
to rise up from the ashes. Before that moment of realization,
however, there stands the pristine white of the architect's drawing
board, a *tabula rasa* on which one can already see a diagrammed
city of light capable of dispelling centuries of darkness and
anxiety. In the ancient cadence of a litany, Le Corbusier bids
utopia arise from the tomb of the past:

> A new world: a high speed world.
> A new life: the machine age.
> A new ideal: use of the machine to liberate the
>   individual.
> A new daily round: productive, recuperative,
>   joyful, healthy: the daily round of machine-
>   age man in the radiant city.
> New cities for old.

But who is it, finally, who will speak the word? For someone
with the politics of Le Corbusier the answer is clear. The government alone is extensive enough in its power to reconfigure society

according to genuine human requirements, instead of merely
capitulating to the special interests of the rich or catering to the
easily manipulated appetites of the masses. Of course, we are
not speaking here of some faceless bureauocracy. Rather, Le
Corbusier goes beyond the tired structures of liberal politics,
beyond the exhaustion of the present day, to a far more ancient,
even mythic notion of power: a patriarchal authority who will
take charge of the present as a father might intervene on behalf
of children he loves. Once again, we realize we have been here
before, whether it be with Plato's philosopher-king, or Utopus,
or the enlightened guardians of Bellamy's America in the year
2000. We recognize the recurrent dream of the wise ruler who
can look into the hearts of his people, identify their true needs,
and then educate them properly. What the world needs, says
Le Corbusier, is a despot—not some benign tyrant such as Plato
hoped to find, but an all-encompassing idea of order, "correct,
realistic, exact."

> This Plan has been drawn up well away from the frenzy
> of the mayor's offices or the town hall, from the cries
> of the electorate or the laments of society's victims. It
> has been drawn up by serene and lucid minds. It has
> taken account of nothing but human truths. It has
> ignored all current regulations, all existing usages and
> channels. . . . *It is a biological creation destined for
> human beings and capable of being realized by modern
> techniques.*

In one sense this cooly daring proposal is an *apologia* for his
own work. There is little doubt that the benevolent despot for
whom the world stands in need is none other than *The Radiant
City* itself, the product of Le Corbusier's own serene and lucid
mind. Thus, while our attention is drawn to the "correct,
realistic, exact" solution to our problems, credit must ultimately be given to the visionary of the ideal city, the human power of
mind that stands behind the despot and from which, in the last
analysis, it is indistinguishable. Small wonder, then, that Le
Corbusier should dedicate his work "à l'Authorité." For however
much he keeps us looking at the prospect of high-rise apartment

towers and rooftop gardens, *l'état, c'est lui.* If you seek his monument, you have only to look around you.

This reference to the Planner, however, is only implicit. What the passage emphasizes is the Plan itself, a total solution characterized by an "indispensable harmony" so finely tuned that it must be accepted in its entirety if the design is to work. All of this is, of course, traditional utopian fare, but it has a certain air of ruthlessness that seems to go beyond the inevitably uncompromising air of any manifesto. We are used to utopia requiring its population to forsake all other visions and cleave only unto its own. But always the acceptance took place, as it were, off-stage, long before the visitor walks on the scene. Here we contemplate somewhat more openly the imposition of the Plan, as its sweeping hand, unrestrained by lesser (or other) considerations than its own, brushes aside custom, constitution, existing government, even the people themselves (whether heard in the "cries of the electorate or the laments of society's victims"). Nothing is allowed to stand in the way.

Le Corbusier everywhere insists that the keystone of his Radiant City is the liberty of the individual. Authority is meant to have a human face, to take into account "nothing but human truths," and to preach the good news to the captives. His sweeping hand has our best interests at heart and is aware of the dangers it risks ("We shall be driven to despair by the uniformity of everything! Yes, it is a danger."). But given the very best of intentions, what one notes in Le Corbusier's presentation of the Plan is the way it has ceased to be an *idea* of the "good place" and become nothing less than a natural law, "a biological creation destined for human beings." No longer a subject for discussion and modification, it appears to be the predestined next step in human development; one can as easily say no to it as deny the force of gravity. In the end the Plan comes to resemble a juggernaut intent on its own fulfillment: a Machine Age fantasy of absolute power which, in all its lucidity of calculation and indifference to cry or lament, chills us to the bone. To a frightening extent, it is no respecter of persons whatsoever.

And for this reason, as perhaps always in utopia, there are no personal choices to be made; the Plan has already made them for us. In the new metropolis, in chains of apartment towers that will

snake across the Paris of tomorrow, 2,700 people will use one
front door. Once over the threshold of their apartments, the
citizens of the Radiant City will find themselves in a self-
contained, soundproofed cell, impervious to the outside, so that
"even a hermit in the depths of a forest could not be more cut
off." Le Corbusier notes that while these apartments are specifically designed for the working class, "in the present state of the
Western world, the one person who won't want to live in them
is the worker! He has not been educated, he is not ready to live
in such apartments." (The Planner also confesses to loving his
Louis XIV townhouse, and with no apparent irony at all). But
the point is that, like it or not, the philosopher-architect knows
what kind of housing will ultimately satisfy our true needs, knows
how best to eliminate the noise and confusion of the marketplace
(and with it "thousands of little private businesses"), knows how
to replace private (French!) cooking with massive catering depart-
ments that will deliver "hot meals in insulated containers to any
apartment on a given block." There is, in fact, nothing that he
does not seem to know.

To some extent this assurance is a feature of all utopian
imagining, which perhaps requires the Planner's total confidence
in the perfection of the design in order to keep waging utopia's
ongoing war against the world as it is. Nonetheless, what is
missing from Le Corbusier's manifesto—an absence which sets
off his twentieth-century scheme for renewal from all the earlier
ones we have considered—is some notion of transcendence. The
idea that whatever the Plan may be, it is at its best an approxima-
tion of God's ideal of human flourishing, is utterly foreign. Every
other system we have looked at thus far is to some degree an
open one. Thus Plato's philosopher-king keeps his attention
forever fixed on the divine forms no human commonwealth
can ever fully realize, while Thomas More's pre-Christian Utopians
pray that they may conform their society to God's eternal gover-
nance. Even Bellamy's up-to-date Bostonians in the year 2000
dial a sermon and link the brotherhood of man to the fatherhood
of God. But in Le Corbusier's Radiant City there is no church to
be found, not so much as a nondescript "meditation room," no
place in the Plan to consider whether human reason, will, vision,
and "truth" might possibly participate in a mystery beyond
humanity. The Planner of the twentieth-century metopolis (as

opposed to the Corbusier who would in two decades time design the magnificent church at Ronchamp) is entirely self-enclosed in a world of his own making. Deliberately breaking with the past, guided by a notion of transcendence that acknowledges only the horizontal plane despite the soaring of its towers, the Radiant City has no referent beyond itself. Of all the new worlds we have looked at, therefore, it is in one sense the "bravest." It lives in the universe completely on its own.

* * *

Strong as utopian self-confidence may be, it is highly vulnerable to sudden deflation by reality. Certainly Le Corbusier's expectations of a golden Machine Age were painfully confounded by the actual events that followed quick upon the publication of *The Radiant City* in 1935. The rise of Nazism in Germany and the Stalinist regime in the Soviet Union, with the Ultimate Solution of the one and the murderous Five Year Plans of the other, made the vision of a benignly despotic utopia capable of realization by modern techniques seem more like a nightmare come true than the fulfillment of a cherished dream. Having paid the price of its own success, utopia ceased to be a noun of plausible hope or of impossible fantasy—becoming instead a dirty word.[27] In short time history showed what faith in a "reign of intelligence," advanced technology, and the strategies of "serene and lucid minds" could actually mean in terms of sheer human misery. To the amazement of a century born to believe in the same progress of reason which Bellamy celebrates in *Looking Backward*, the impulse toward institutionalized perfection and an allegiance to "nothing but human truths" had joined to create a monster that perhaps no one could have foreseen, at least not without some notion of human sin to raise a warning. And so in a bitterly ironic turn of events, the solution had become the problem, the liberator the enemy, the total cure a sickness unto death. As Nicholas Berdyaev wrote in *Slavery and Freedom*—a passage which Aldous Huxley would use as an epigraph to his 1932 novel, *Brave New World*—

> Utopias seem very much more realizable than we
> formerly supposed. And now we find ourselves facing

> a question which is painful in a new kind of way: How
> to avoid their realization? . . . Perhaps a new age is
> beginning, an age in which the intellectuals and the
> cultivated class will dream of methods of avoiding
> utopia and of returning to a society that is nonutopian,
> that is less "perfect" and more free.

The dream of how to avoid utopia actually began in the late
nineteenth century as a reaction to *Looking Backward*, whose
appearance in 1888 inspired not only the adulatory Bellamy
Clubs mentioned above, but sharp attack and counter-imagin-
ing.[28] Of far greater power were the anti-utopian fictions written
in the first half of the twentieth century, and in the light of
realized utopian "values," by the same sort of humanist writer
who in earlier age would have felt called upon to plan, rather than
oppose, an ideal commonwealth. The three most noteworthy
are Eugene Zamiatin in *We* (1920), Aldous Huxley in *Brave New
World* (1932), and George Orwell in *1984*, published in 1949, a
year before the author's death.

What joins these writers together, more even than their common revulsion from the totalitarian politics of their time, is a
profound distrust of the utopian enterprise itself. For Berdyaev
the dream is tainted at its source and Plato's Republic nothing
less than "a thorough-going tyranny, a denial of all freedom and
of the value of the personality." The others are perhaps less
sweeping in their condemnation, but nonetheless share his deep-
seated suspicion of any recreation of the world according to
Plan, especially when the design for living is generated by intellectuals without humility or doubt. Suspecting the demand for a
"clean table-cloth" to be a prelude to oppression, these writers
prefer haphazard corruption to ideological purity on the grounds
that it is always less evil in the long run. At whatever cost—even
of happiness—human freedom is more precious to them than
either cleanliness or order. Hence they draw a horrifyingly convincing portrait of what has come to be called "dystopia": the
perfectly awful place that is the ironic outcome of serene and
lucid minds at work. Holding up a mirror to reason's nightmare,
these novelists expose the terrible wages of perfection, the insane
irrationality that can result from any attempt to favor "mind"
over every other human faculty or impulse. Whereas Thomas

More and Edward Bellamy use the contrast of the world as it is
and the world as it might be to argue for the untried possibility,
writers like Zamiatin and Orwell completely reverse this order,
ushering us into a future where the horrors of "after" are far
worse than the troubles of "before."

In making this point, the anti-utopian exalts everything that
traditionally has been excluded or disparaged by the tyranny of
the ideal. The list of things forbidden is, of course, as old as
Plato's proscriptions in the *Republic*: the untamed world of
nature, a vital continuity with the past world, the body and its
unpredictable passions, intimate (and therefore private) relationships, the whole realm of the idiosyncratic and surprising. By
valuing precisely what utopia dismisses as unclean and dangerous,
this profoundly conservative spirit treasures the little pleasures of
human life as one would guard an endangered species, prizing
the merely ordinary as if it were truly precious, vulnerable to
extinction, and a necessary link to our deepest "roots." And so
the opponents of utopia celebrate our freedom to make mistakes
or behave irrationally, to shut doors, to be alone. Nostalgic for
the pre-utopian world, and wary of a future they fear may be
closer at hand than we think, they look to the routine joys and
sorrows of human existence as it has always been—sometimes
brutal, always disorderly, yet lived out in an open world where we
are bound to work out our measure of freedom with fear and
trembling. Prophesying against the "ideal" to come, the anti-
utopian spirit asks us in turn to look backward for our salvation.

This is not to say that these writers are in any traditional
sense "religious," nor to minimize their indictment of Christianity
for providing utopia with demonic models of orthodoxy and
oppression. One might with far more justice refer to them as
romantics untimely born, or as humanists alarmed at the consequences of humanism, than even as fellow-travellers with Christian
critics of utopia. Nonetheless, Zamiatin, Huxley and Orwell in
their different ways all expose the religious impulse within the
twentieth-century rage for order, showing how the post-Enlightenment exaltation of reason has led to a cult of irrational authority.
The philosopher-kings have turned themselves into gods, while
their rejection of any notion of human transcendence has ended
up enslaving humanity in a prison of its own design. With the

removal of God from the Radiant City—and with the departure
of God, all sense of our own creation in the divine image—people
have been left vulnerable to redefinition, reshaping, or to outright elimination. Utopia may have liberated itself from the sense
of sin and accountability, but in doing so it has also deprived
humanity of protection from itself. The ideal commonwealth
has banished God in order to secure its own divinity.

If dystopia is a totalitarian religion demanding absolute
obedience on the part of its faithful, it is easy to see why the
primary strategy of this fiction is to dramatize an act of radical
opposition and disbelief. It tells the story of an individual who
(in Zamiatin's metaphor) hurls a single ounce of "I" against a ton
of "We." Its heroes are men and women who through some dim
remembrance of things past, or leap of imagination, or "seduction" by the forbidden and repressed are inspired to fall out of
step. The result is high treason and apostacy: an individual
refuses to worship a false god, be it the Stalinesque "Well-Doer"
of Zamiatin or Orwell's "Big Brother." Yet this Promethean
gesture does not arise out of extraordinary heroism or courage
or even goodness; it is more like a child's act of defiance, which
by its mere existence in a world without opposition comes to
seem like an epic challenge to the whole utopian order. For this
reason, the individual's act of rebellion, by the sheer fact of its
individuality, is a flaw in the pattern that must be eliminated, a
microbe too pernicious to be left to itself. When the individual
steps out of line the reader is encouraged to hope for the best,
and for a moment it actually seems as if the tiny disruption of
a few persons may serve as a wrench thrown into the works of the
utopian juggernaut. Yet so relentless is the pessimism of these
works, as determined to deny any ray of light as the traditional
utopia is reluctant to admit the cloud on its horizon, that in every
case "I" is crushed by "We," and the ideal order remains
intact. As Zamiatin's hero says, amazed at the prospect of
fighting back, "You, versus the United State! It's the same as if
you were to cover the muzzle of a gun with your hands and
expect that way to prevent the shot."

Because anti-utopian fiction portrays the triumph of evil,
which has always engaged the imagination far more than the
good, it is at once spell-binding reading and difficult to take. Its
purpose, however, is not to plunge the reader into despair, even

though imprisonment in the abyss is exactly the fate which each portrayal of dystopia places before us. Rather, it wants to exaggerate what it perceives to be the dangers of the present and, in order to highlight their importance, draw them out to their logical consequences. By creating a horror, in other words, these novels mean to leave us with a warning. Although picturing the absolutely hopeless, their appeal is to people who have not been crushed or lobotomized or driven to suicide (to cite the ends which befall the heroes of Orwell, Zamiatin, and Huxley respectively); they reach out to the reader who is still free. Rather than asking us to welcome the future with an open embrace, they encourage us to arm ourselves against it while we still can. Theirs is most profoundly a literature of prevention.

Given the doom that ultimately prevails in fiction of this kind, it is easy to miss its essentially satiric thrust, that dark humor which Nikolai Gogol characterized as "laughter through tears." Just as utopia is meant to render our everyday world grotesque and ridiculous, so too will the portrayal of dystopia distort the "ideal" commonwealth into a very bad joke indeed. As Zamiatin's protagonist observes, "Laughter is the most terrible of weapons; you can kill anything with laughter, even murder." This never turns out literally to be the case because murder of one kind of another always has the final say. But it nonetheless points to the double strategy of these works, which join a *reductio ad absurdum* to the tactics of fear.

This satirical thrust is especially strong in Zamiatin's novel, which on one level reads like a spoof of *The Radiant City* even as it is a prophetic denunciation of Moscow's "reign of intelligence." Born in 1884, just three years before Le Corbusier, and trained in Russia as a mathematician and engineer, Zamiatin also experienced a short-lived euphoria at the prospect of Machine Age evolution and the triumph of revolution.[29] His extraordinarily provocative *We*, which deserves a much wider acquaintance than it has enjoyed thus far, was written in 1920 and first came out in America four years later. Looking forward almost a thousand years beyond *Looking Backward*, to a "United State" that shares some features of the international socialism that Bellamy prophesied, the novel protrays the post-Enlightenment utopia as a dream come true— with a vengeance. It introduces us to life within the Radiant City as it might turn out to be.

Zamiatin depicts for us a precision-made utopia that has achieved for its citizens a "mathematically faultless happiness." Under a sky of flawless blue, it stretches out before us as Le Corbusier's renovated Paris might look if the architect had his way: "the impeccably straight streets, the glistening glass of the pavement, the divine parallelepipeds, the square harmony." Living within this utopian bubble is a population of "numbers": human beings who make up the grand equation that *is* the United State by forming individual cells within a "powerful organization of millions." Regulated to the second over the course of each day, the citizens form a single mechanism which at a fore-ordained moment lifts spoon to mouth, foot to pavement, pen to paper. It is no wonder, therefore, that everyone's favorite reading is a venerable classic from the old days, "that greatest of all monuments, the Official Railroad Guide."

It is precisely this regulation that constitutes the happy life and accounts for the drastic change in human sensibility that our narrator, D-503, both exemplifies and describes for us. Incorporating elements of radical social reorganization that are to be found in Plato, More and Bellamy, Zamiatin succeeds as none of them did in suggesting what actually it might be like to be utopia's new Adam and think with a "renewed mind." A sense of this mind is partially revealed through examples of D-503's revulsion against the past, as he expresses his disgust for that vanished world which left sexual life absolutely without control, when anyone able to do so produced children outside conformity to maternal and paternal norms, or permitted people to live in "strange opaque dwellings" rather than behind transparent glass walls, "beneath the eyes of everyone, always bathed in light"— with a discrete curtain drawn only when duly registered partners come to make a sexual transaction.

More evocative still are the spontaneous reactions that reveal D-503's inner workings: his revulsion from any curved line, his appreciation of dance because of its *unfree* movement. Through D-503 we see how feelings can be formulated or factored out entirely—how reason can become a matter of computation. So convincing is Zamiatin's evocation of this "renewed mind," moreover, that after only a few pages the reader begins to understand why D-503 can dismiss a simple feeling of pity as an "arithmetical ignorance," while the very idea of a personal "right" is dissolved in an instant by the acid of reason. Such ideas and feelings, which constitute our own sense of what it means to be human, have come to be looked upon in the United State as a throwback to the primitive chaos of the past—a jarring note of discord that D-503 describes, with a shameful glance at the embarassing hair on his own hands, as "the echo of the apes."

At the control board of the United State is a figure who, in a world where men and women are known only by a single letter and number, uniquely bears a name. The "Well-Doer" is a composite of Plato's philosopher-king, More's Utopus, Bellamy's Guardians, Le Corbusier's Authority, as well as a dreadful prophecy of Adolf Hitler and Joseph Stalin. But perhaps his most important prototype is the figure of the Grand Inquisitor who, as presented in the legend which Ivan tells Alyosha in Dostoevsky's *The Brothers Karamazov*, comes to cast a long shadow over much of twentieth-century literature. In Dostoevsky's legend a high minister of the Spanish Inquisition berates Christ for having rejected the offerings of Satan (miracle, mystery and authority) in favor of that burden with which the great mass of people has never been able to live—freedom. To correct Christ's error, the Inquisitor and his church have taken away individual choice by an imposition of authority under the guise of miracle and mystery. It is an exchange that has brought about peace and happiness, a life without struggle and uncertainty, unburdened by the terrible legacy of Eden: the knowledge of good and evil. Out of a desire to make things easier for people (as well as leaving them more susceptible to control), the authorities have created a human ant-hill in which the unthinking masses can find refuge from the torment of personal decision and private responsibility. To be sure, the Inquisitor himself knows the pain of free will, and carries with him an awareness of what the masses have been delivered from—the solitude of Christ in the wilderness or alone upon the cross. But like a loving parent who knows his offspring cannot bear very much reality, he has taken that suffering upon himself so that his children may know only the happiness of mindless living. He has, in effect, placed humanity back in the garden, in a state of primal innocence.

Zamiatin's Well-Doer is a kinsman of the Grand Inquisitor, and a parody of that figure of patriarchal authority which has haunted our imagination ever since Plato suggested him in the

Republic: austere, solitary, dedicated to the best interests of humanity, denying self in order to make us happy. Acting as the "New Jehovah" of this hi-tech Eden, he presides over a society in which freedom has been recognized as the original sin, and therefore as the source of all crime against the happy life. Because the urge to transgression has remained a trouble in this paradise, the Well-Doer must occasionally resort to the enforced (and lethal) penance of "The Machine"—an enormous bell jar in which offenders against the Plan, in a grotesque version of Bellamy's solitary confinement for those who refuse the Industrial Army, slowly and torturously lose the right to breathe. Such acts of recrimination are all by way of weeding out the garden. For, as the "poet laureate" friend of D-503 remarks, in language that brings Zamiatin's theological frame of reference to the fore: "Paradise again! We returned to the simple-mindedness and innocence of Adam and Eve. No more meddling with good and evil and all that; everything is simple again, heavenly, childishly simple!" He suggests what we might have to leave behind us in order to get ourselves back into the innocence of Eden.

The story Zamiatin's novel tells, however, is of no paradise regained; instead, it is a retelling of the Fall, the seduction of utopia's second Adam by another Eve. The woman exposes D-503 to "soul," a disease that so infects him with the desire for secrecy and rebellion that he joins with others to tear down the walls that enclose utopia, and thereby open it to everything that has escaped its control. Their act of resistance grows to epidemic proportions, as if "soul" could reclaim its life-giving hold upon human being once again. But what finally restores the status quo is the Well-Doer's discovery of a cure, both scientific and fool-proof, to maintain the undisturbed ignorance of Eden. By a simple removal of the soul's festering splinter, an untying of its knot, society can produce an ideal (which is to say, lobotomized) citizen. It can make its people happy by the simple act of elim-inating what makes them human. As the Well-Doer says to D-503,

> I ask: what was it that man from his diaper age
> dreamed of, tormented himself for, prayed for? He
> longed for that day when someone would tell him what
> happiness is, and then would chain him to it. What else
> are we doing now? The ancient dream about a para-

dise. . . . Remember: there in paradise they know no
desires any more, no pity, no love; there they all are—
blessed. An operation has been performed upon their
center of fancy; that is why they are blessed, angels,
servants of God.

This account of the Well-Doer's ultimate solution reads like a
travesty of realized eschatology. For what he has achieved by a
simple maneuver of X-rays is a grotesque version of the blessed
life envisioned by St. John the Divine in the New Jerusalem
("Neither shall there be mourning nor crying nor pain any more"),
and prophesied from of old by the prophet Ezekiel ("A new
heart I will give you, and a new spirit I will put within you").
Conversion of heart, renewal of mind, a new heaven and a new
earth: all these transcendent gifts of God promised to humanity
throughout the long course of Scripture have been taken over.
The Well-Doer has made all the ancient dreams come true, has
told his creatures, "REJOICE! For from now on we are *perfect*!"
Chained to happiness in a paradise they will never want to leave,
his humanoid numbers want only to add up to his totalitarian
sum, to serve him all their days. He has made a more reliable
product than any previous god-player.

* * *

Utopia had always argued that the enlightened few, if given
absolute power, would guide and direct the well-being of all.
What George Orwell portrays in *1984*, however, is the dire consequences of this possession: absolute and unmitigated corruption.
He introduces into his analysis the single human factor which
utopian thinkers have always assumed they could get the better
of—the reality of evil. Beyond even the dimensions of Zamiatin's
nightmare, to which his novel owes an enormous debt, he shows
how intelligence can turn itself to evil as easily as to good; how
perhaps it is even more "natural" for the powerful to choose the
former than the latter. Without any Grand Inquisitorial pretense
on the part of its leaders that their repressive measures are only
intended to make the people happy or good, *1984* shows a society
in which power is an end in itself, whose population exists only to
be controlled. "Imagine," Winston Smith is asked, "a boot

stamping on a human face—forever." Just as hell, like evil, is
traditionally defined as the absence of good, so the boundless
realm of Oceania is "nowhere" on the map of utopia. A republic
without justice, a commonwealth without commonality, it is the
negative face of a dream that may have always contained the
elements of its own negation. For if utopia represents the insti-
tutionalization of goodness for the enhancement of our humanity, Orwell's world exemplifies nothing less than a violent return
of what has been repressed. He shows us the irrational institution-
alization of evil under rational disguise, in which human nature
has been so "redefined" as almost no longer to exist.

The massive redefinition of personality which Orwell imagines
taking place in a mere matter of decades (as opposed to Zamiatin's
millennial projections of human "computerization") builds, once
again, on venerable utopian foundations. Given its belief in the
essential malleability of human beings, utopian schemes have
always sought ways in which to transform selfish and self-
destructive individuals into conscientious members of a community which claims their primary allegiance. It is always the same:
the group must increase, while the individual decreases. Whether
by peer shaming or official praise or, more extensively still, by
a radical restructuring of the social environment, its aim is always
to produce better citizens. What we see in *1984*, therefore, is
a version of that moulding of consciousness which we have been
considering ever since Raphael Hytholoday's rhapsody on what
King Utopus managed to accomplish: "In Utopia all greed for
money was entirely removed with the use of money! What a mass
of troubles was then cut away! What a crop of crimes was then
pulled up by the roots!" Oceania has also embarked upon a program of extirpation, except what it is in the process of removing is
individuality itself. It is the notion of a person as an autonomous
entity, possessed of a self which is unique and precious, that is
being pulled up by the roots.

To this end, the sole thrust of technological advance in *1984*
is toward the elimination of the private response. Gone is the
excitement of a Bellamy over the radio-telephone, or of a Le
Corbusier over the sleek proficiency of his urban "machine for
living." Instead, Orwell gives us the telescreen, and with it the
prospect of constant surveillance and review as technology assists
the Party's Thought Police in ferreting out any eccentricity, any

private act, any deviation from an arbitrarily imposed (and constantly shifting) norm. The result is a mass of human beings who
are entirely encased by "protective stupidity"; who live under
conditions of carefully controlled insanity designed to turn what
was a complex and potentially recalcitrant individual into a living
telescreen—a passive, unreflective surface on which the Party may
project its own image and likeness. From childhood on they
undergo an elaborate mental training, formal and environmental
alike, that makes the Party member not only unwilling but unable
to think. Since Big Brother is always watching, and has already
devised scientific means to search the unspoken heart, survival
depends on inward vacancy as well as outward conformity. "A
Party member is expected to have no private emotions and no
respites from enthusiasm." As in Zamiatin's *We*, it is lethal to
have a soul.

The world Orwell describes is an exaggeration of twentieth-
century totalitarianism, an extreme fiction with the compelling
verisimilitude of truth.[30] In what amounts to a very frightening
kind of satire, the hairline cracks or open fissures of the post-war
period become enormous fault lines running through the body
politic, great chasms into which human reality as we have always
known it has plunged. The globe is divided into three totalitarian
regimes—Oceania, Eurasia, and Eastasia—all of which are virtually
indistinguishable. These superpowers are engaged in constant
conflict, two at a time, with sides being changed without warning—and even in the middle of a political harangue. People are
kept under a martial law that is never lifted, in a state of constant
crisis which always requires repression. And so the citizens of
Oceania are divided and conquered by their own government,
which uses its continual war powers to keep the structure of
society intact and itself in control.

We see none of the material plenty that the technological
breakthroughs of the century might lead us to expect. This is
partly because the mindless vacancy required for social conformity does not lend itself to invention or discovery. Cogs do not
invent machines. But it is also true that the means of production have been wholly geared to the making of war—against the
"enemy" abroad, of course, but also against every manifestation
of independence at home—and therefore are entirely self-
consuming. And so instead of the antiseptic world of glass and

steel which Le Corbusier planned and Zamiatin foretold, the
capital city in which the story unfolds, the "London" of yester-
year, is found sinking ever deeper into the almost Dickensian
decay which inspired such revulsion in the author of *The Radiant
City*—a dark helter-skelter labyrinth of alleys, pubs, and rubble.
The only interruptions in the bleakness of this dreary cityscape
are the four massive buildings which, like the public palaces of
Bellamy's Boston in the year 2000, dominate the horizon. They
are the Ministries of Truth, Peace, Love, and Plenty, known
respectively in the official language of the future—"Newspeak"—
as Minitrue, Minipax, Miniluv, and Miniplenty.

The etymology of these names goes to the cold heart of *1984*.
"Mini" stands most obviously for ministry, and seems at first
like an example of the acronyms and abbreviations that we have
come to endure in our own public sector. And yet "mini," at
least in "Oldspeak," has another association as well: it is short
for "minimum," an indication of the smallest possible quantity
of something. The Newspeak word offers, therefore, a double
entendre: Minitrue is both the Ministry of Truth *and* it advances
truth's minimum. That this is indeed the case is borne out by the
nature of Winston Smith's job there. For as we come to see,
Minitrue is the center of propaganda and news control where
hundreds of lesser Party workers like Smith, under close and constant supervision, "process" the past, bring it up to date with the
line of the moment, or eliminate it entirely in the incinerators that
daily consume society's memory. The Ministry bears the same
minimal relation to truth as Miniluv, the windowless tower of
punishment and torture, bears to love.

On the facades of these massive buildings we read the slogan
of the Party: "War is Peace. Freedom is Slavery. Ignorance is
Strength." These three lapidary sentences, simple and declarative,
have about them the aura of rationality, as if they were a short
manifesto of Enlightenment civilization—like "Liberté, Egalité,
Fraternité." In fact they make no sense at all, at least by received
notions of logic and contradiction. "War" and "Peace," which
represent antithetical realities, here become interchangeable when
brought together by an utterly insubstantial and meaningless "is."
Under the guise of rationality, the Party has in fact subverted
reason, and with it any sense of objectivity or fact. Two and two
can as easily make five as four, because nowhere is there any hard

notion of truth; even sanity is only a matter of statistics. And yet
so consistent is this madness that the reader comes to see its
method, comes even to see that the Party's slogan is quite accurately descriptive of life in Oceania. Constant warfare *is* the
Party's way of maintaining civil peace; ignorance, the means by
which the social order is kept static and the Party in control;
freedom, known only in that utter loss of self-determination that
we acknowledge to be slavery.

Beneath both ranks of Party membership is the vast majority
of the population who, like the squalid districts in which they
live, exist in the shadow of the public ministries. These are the
"proles," who form the mainstay of every crowd scene and military troop. They escape the telescreen surveillance imposed on all
Party members simply by having no power to abuse and no
conduct worth investigating. Winston Smith fantasizes throughout
the novel that the future belongs to them. He is drawn to their
quarters, where in the midst of cheap "Victory" gin, phony
lotteries and furtive pleasures, he not only finds himself in the
presence of a somewhat more genuine (if equally hopeless) humanity, but in contact with his own. The proles remind him of the
past.

One of Orwell's constant themes is Oceania's unrelenting
assault on the world that preceded it—an assault by which the
Party hopes to eliminate all point of comparison between its own
regime and any former one. But in this program of oblivion we
also see the desire of all utopias to break with history, whether by
separating from the cultural mainstream and its tainted inheritance
or by so denigrating the past that its memory inspires only pity and
disdain. History, after all, is notoriously unclean; utopia wants in
some sense to wash its hands of the whole business. In Orwell's
vision of the future, however, any act of looking backward, even
in disgust and disapproval, is discouraged. It is also fast on the
way to becoming impossible. Not only are records of the past
being systematically destroyed (book by book, clipping by
clipping), but the living vehicle of its conservation—language—is
being cut loose from its moorings, severed from the world that
used to be and therefore from the range of thought, feeling, and
value it makes available.

The development of "Newspeak" is Orwell's prime case in
point, for in the forefront of Oceania's plan to create a new and

radically ahistorical human nature is its deconstruction of the
word.[31] Newspeak represents a stringently "sanitized" English,
empty of color, nuance, and associations with the former age.
Indeed, it is shorn of associations of any kind, being a severely
diminished mode of human communication designed precisely
with the intent of diminishing the humanity of the speaker. In
particular, Newspeak aims to inhibit the ability of a person to
say anything that will evoke the emotional and spiritual options
of past times or in any way challenge the status quo established
by the Party. With the loss of an ability to speak subversively
will also go the power to think or even feel at variance with
what is constantly being redefined as reality. It is the goal of the
Party to create new language, with the specific intent of making
a new human being. Words are invented that express the peculiar
mode of "thought" the Party wants to encourage. For instance,
there is the noun "doublethink," which more than any other
Newspeak word conveys what is intended to pass for mental
activity: "To know and not to know, to be conscious of complete
truthfulness while telling carefully constructed lies, to hold
simultaneously two opinions which cancel out, knowing them to
be contradictory and believing in both of them, to use logic
against logic. . . ." American readers in the wake of 1984 can
make their own connections to this linguistic phenomenon by
recalling our current language of duplicity, which uses "neutral-
ize" for murder and "misinformation" for lie.

But aside from its use of language both to express and to
inculcate its own realities, Newspeak is primarily a process of
elimination by which the humane values of the past are to be
phased out of existence or swallowed up entirely by the single
omnibus noun intended to cover (and cover up) the varied options
offered by Oldspeak English: the word "crimethink." By the
mid-twenty-first century, when Newspeak is expected to be not
only the official language of the Party but the only way to com-
municate in Oceania, a familiar line from Shakespeare, such as
Polonius's charge to Hamlet, "To thine own self be true," will be
(in both senses of the word) unspeakable. To begin with, it will
be incapable of expression in a language which, like the society
that invented it, has no equivalent for "thine own" or "self" or
"true." Secondly, even if Polonius's line could be translated by
"crimethink," it would be unspeakable in the sense of hateful

or objectionable. It would be at once nonsensical and forbidden.
Thus it is the Party's hope to create a new Adam for whom
"truth to self" will be not only an unintelligible notion, but
one worthy to be considered a capital offense. If *Hamlet* could
ever see a Newspeak production, therefore, it would be a one-
word play—its five acts reduced to a single noun, "crimethink"—
and its actors, director, producer and audience hauled off to
Miniluv for after-theater "discussion." A new language for a new
humanity.

The narrative action of *1984* unfolds in three distinct movements. In the initial section we watch as Winston Smith gradually
comes to separate himself from the Party, first through secret
"thoughtcrime" hidden during his work at the Ministry of Truth,
then in the illicit purchase of a diary, and gradually in the sensual
pleasure and affection he discovers with another Party member—
a woman known to us only as Julia—who defies the sexual repression of the "new and happy life" by becoming a rebel from
the waist downward. In the novel's second movement this
increment of rebellion, expressed primarily in terms of an intense
personal relationship and a forbidden hideaway in the prole
quarters, culminates in the ultimate act of definance: political
opposition to the state. The couple offer themselves in service to
the outlawed "Brotherhood" and promise it the total allegiance
once claimed by the Party. But there is no hiding from Big
Brother. Winston and Julia are captured in their little room above
a "curiosity" shop, the place where, ironically, they thought to
find themselves in touch with a more humane past (symbolized by
the cherished anachronism of the room's double bed) and to be
safe from the otherwise omnipresent telescreen. From behind an
engraving of the Church of St. Clement's Dane nailed to the wall,
however, they have been watched and listened to. Their sanctuary
turns out to have been a screening room all along.

In the third and final section, Winston is dragged from his
hideaway and taken to the Ministry of Love, where he is tortured
by the same O'Brien who brought him into the Brotherhood. In
the end his resistance is overwhelmed and his self eliminated. We
never know if the Brotherhood truly exists, or whether it is, after
all, the Party's own fifth column, its ruse to ferret out dissidents
in order to crush them. Nor do we learn if Big Brother is more
than a "supreme fiction," or, if he does exist, if he and O'Brien
are actually one and the same. All our hopes have been dashed,

including the one that looks for answers to such questions. But
so despairing is the novel in conclusion that somehow it does not
matter very much what the truth is, or whether it can ever be
obtained.

What Orwell shows to have befallen Winston is equivalent in
effect to the neutron bomb: his body remains standing but his
soul is dead. In an awful parody of utopian "rebirth," every shred
of self-respect is unravelled, every impulse to withhold or disagree
become dysfunctional. Even the few centimeters within the skull
which he once thought were forever his own have been annexed
completely by the Party. As O'Brien tells him, "You will be
hollow. We shall squeeze you empty, and then we shall fill you
with ourselves." On the basis of what Orwell gives us, this predic-
tion turns out to be the terrible truth once Winston has undergone
the horrors of "Room 101" (dystopia's point of no return) and
been liberated for slavery. With dreadful symmetry, the act of
personal rebellion that formally began with his first diary entry,

> DOWN WITH BIG BROTHER
> DOWN WITH BIG BROTHER
> DOWN WITH BIG BROTHER
> DOWN WITH BIG BROTHER
> DOWN WITH BIG BROTHER

is balanced by a complete reversal in the novel's closing paragraph.
For there we see Winston "squeezed dry" indeed, adoring the
Party's collective face on the telescreen and in that adoration
revering everything he once loathed and hurled himself against.

> He gazed up at the enormous face. Forty years it
> had taken to learn what kind of smile was hidden
> beneath the dark moustache. O cruel, o needless mis-
> understanding! O stubborn self-willed exile from the
> loving breast! Two gin-scented tears trickled down from
> the side of his nose. But it was all right, everything was
> all right, the struggle was finished. He had won the
> victory over himself. He loved Big Brother.

That people can be reshaped to fit a notion of ideal humanity,
taught to cooperate with their society for the purpose of bringing

about a "new and happy life," and that a single leader or an elite
can break with the past in order to create a more orderly and
harmonious world for the future are all convictions that we have
observed, with amazingly little variation, from Plato to Le
Corbusier. In the imagination of Zamiatin and Orwell, however,
these ideals are shown to conceal a totalitarian impulse which,
under the right conditions, can lead to the destruction of humanity rather than to its flourishing. They remind us how easily
reason can become ruthless rationalization and of how problem-
atic a gift intelligence can be when it is not guided by mercy and
love. After all, the same serene and lucid mind that can plan a
Radiant City can also turn a shining tower of technological
achievement into the Ministry of Love.

If the primary feature of this anti-utopian literature is its
obsession with evil, then Orwell goes quite beyond his peers.
There is no apology for tyranny—what Zamiatin's Well-Doer proclaims to be "an algebraic love for humanity [that] must inevitably be inhuman." No, in *1984* we find ourselves completely
cut loose from the Grand Inquisitor passage, with its discussion
of happiness at the expense of freedom. In a new twist on
Zamiatin and Huxley, love and truth have been entirely collapsed
into cruelty. "We are not interested in the good of others," says
O'Brien, "we are interested only in power." One recalls the image
of the human face crushed forever. It is as if in this still spell-
binding novel the dark glass of dystopia had reached a shattering
point in its attempt to imagine the full perversity of the utopian
mind.

But it is not of evil alone that Orwell reminds us. There is also
the manifold world of experience that stands outside the Party's
grip, where beauty and particularity escape detection and in so
doing suggest the possibility of freedom. One thinks of the April
countryside into which Winston and Julia take refuge for a day—
a traditional pastoral landscape in which thrushes sing (as
Zamiatin's novel would have it) not "because of" but only "just
so." There is also the glass paper weight that Winston treasures for
its fragile bit of coral imbedded at the center, or his glimpse of a
prole woman hanging up her family's wash in a filthy alley—a
woman "blown up to monstrous proportions by childbearing, then
hardened, roughened by work," yet undeniably beautiful in her
earthiness. But most important of all, there exists in each person

an interior world of dreams, association, and fancy which constitutes the individual self. Winston calls this rich interior space his
"Golden Country," and from its vantage feels it possible "to
annihilate a whole culture, a whole system of thought, as though
Big Brother and the Party and the Thought Police could all be
swept away into nothingness."

Of course, in the world of the novel this is precisely what he
cannot do. Every exit is blocked and there are no corners left
in which to hide. In the end, there is not even a self in which to
keep the "Golden Country" alive. This sense of doom is what
Orwell's novel is noted for even now, more than thirty-five years
after its publication and in the wake of the year 1984 which it
made so ominous for us. In this period of time it has become one
of those contemporary classics, like Kafka's far greater work,
The Trial, which we use to frighten ourselves—as if our fear might
somehow protect us from Big Brother and all his works. In a
way, we have taken it as a blueprint of the future rather than as
a metaphoric "nowhere" in whose imagined territory we may
better sort out the values and priorities of real places in which we
live. In party conversation or on television or in the newspaper,
we have asked ourselves if, after all, "it" might be coming true.

But perhaps the real value of novels like *We* and *1984* lies not
in their fantastic predictions, but in their effort to both celebrate
and secure what they regard as most precious in human existence
right now. They remind us that we are constantly in danger of
either damaging or destroying the treasures of ordinary living in
that lust to control experience which has always been the hall-
mark of utopian dreamers. In the broadest sense of the term,
these treasures offer us an *ecological* warning—a call to conserve
the "flaw," "stain" and "microbe" which is our individual self,
and without which life would be unendurable.

For the believing reader this literature also provides a peculiar
set of challenges. On the one hand, it would seem to support the
religious critic of culture who rejects that notion which in one
form or another has been current since the Renaissance: the idea
that "man is the measure of all things." When O'Brien says to
Winston, "Outside man there is nothing," he is in one sense only
taking this familiar adage to its logical conclusion and, in fact,
stating the assumptions of many in our own time, albeit in a
wholly perverse context. But as if to give fair warning against the

unintended side effects of this kind of humanism, the work of
anti-utopian imagination constructs a world in which the
"outside" has been banished completely and where every human
prospect is relentlessly horizontal. These cautionary tales suggest
that when a civilization divinizes humanity and proclaims God
dead it is more likely to usher in the reign of Satan than that
secular paradise of a world "come of age." By virtue of their conservativism, their penchant for looking backward with longing,
these novels seem to be written by fellow travellers with the
Christian opponent of modern culture.

But lest the religious-minded falsely appropriate the anti-
utopian witness for their own purpose—as has been the case among
Roman Catholics since the death of the very anti-Catholic George
Orwell[32]—it must be remembered that these thinkers all link the
totalitarian movements of the twentieth century to the age-old
strategies of Christian indoctrination and repression. For both
Zamiatin and Orwell (as for Dostoevsky before them), the
religious establishment has taught the elementary lessons in
cruelty, mind control and the mentality of the ant hill. *1984*'s
Room 101 traces its origins to the Inquisitor's torture chamber.
Now Christians may very well deal with this criticism by chalking
it up to corruption within the church or, as the appeal of last
resort, by recourse to the doctrine of original sin. Nonetheless
anti-utopian imagination can be helpful not only in curbing the
arrogance of those who would remake us and our society into
their fantasy of human flourishing, but also by offering the
believer a caveat to consider. Let those who think they know
what the New Jerusalem looks like approach their vision with
caution—and in the spirit of that special aspect of humility which
is doubt.

getting somewhere

It may be that we have reached a point where utopia is no longer
a viable dream. In a century which has seen two world wars,
Hitler's Solution and a succession of Soviet Plans, along with the
terrible consequences of much technological "advance," we are a
great deal more wary than our forebears. We may also be con-
siderably more selfish. The whole notion of public service now
has an air of quaintness that stands in vivid contrast to the private
pursuits we cultivate more naturally. Although prophets are
always without honor in their own lands, it is especially hard to
imagine a Hythloday commanding any attention in ours, let alone
a Sir Thomas More called to the inner circle of power to advise
his prince. Bellamy's belief in progress has been rather thoroughly
discredited, while more often than not Le Corbusier's vision of
the *ville radieuse* has turned into the monstrous banality of so
much urban construction. Certainly in the rhetoric of American
politics we have followed a trajectory that reaches for less: from
New Deal to Fair Deal to New Frontier to Great Society to
Jimmy Carter's "Dream"—only to settle in 1984 for a more or
less enlightened self-interest. For us the "good place" may begin
(and end) only at home.[33]
    And yet in the same period that would seem to have rejected
even the idea of utopia as either too dangerous or too naive, we
find two postwar reworkings of the grand old tradition. B.F.
Skinner's *Walden Two* (1948) and Aldous Huxley's palinodic
Island (1962) both stake their hopes for a more fulfilling human
existence on the same science of human conditioning from which
Zamiatin and Orwell and the Huxley of *Brave New World* drew
back in such horror.[34] Not surprisingly, both works retreat from
the global claims of *Looking Backward*, placing their hopes
instead on the manageably-sized, relatively isolated communities
favored by earlier utopian thinkers. They also argue against
Orwell that the happy life is indeed ours to program: behaviorism

is their hope for the future. Moreover, for Skinner and Huxley
the benign conditioning of utopia may be the *only* thing that
saves us from extinction. Like Le Corbusier they ask why, if we
can mobilize for global death, we cannot plan instead for life—
for the flourishing that may very well lie beyond our mere
survival.

B.F. Skinner's novel, like *1984*, has come to signify the
furthest development of the utopian imagination in our time;
to some, even its debasement and virtual extinction.[35] It opens
with two recently discharged servicemen who have just returned
from combat with questions about their own futures. They ask a
university professor named Burris why they need take up where
they left off before the army. Isn't it time for a fresh beginning?
"Why not get some people together and set up a social system
somewhere that will really work?" By chance they learn of a
community founded by a former friend of Burris and only a day's
journey away. Together with their girlfriends, Burris and another
professor named Castle, they work their way to the world of T.E.
Frazier—the founding father of Walden Two and a mouthpiece
for Skinner's own views. What they go on to find there is a
society of nearly one thousand people, who live prosperously but
without private wealth; who work, but only a reasonable amount;
who have substituted mutual cooperation for cut-throat competi-
tion.

For us, their discovery is familiar territory. And indeed, the
one sceptic in the group, Professor Castle, who has taught a
course at the university on utopian literature "from Plato and
More and Bacon's New Atlantis down to *Looking Backward* and
even Shangri-La," frequently reminds us that so much of what we
encounter there is of a piece with this tradition. What separates
Walden Two from the utopian dreams of the past, however, is
more than its claim to be already happening. Its novelty does not
lie in Frazier's goals for the happy life, for we have encountered
them all before: physical health, steady but minimal work, the
chance to exercise talents and interests, an opportunity to make
decent relationships with other people, time for rest and recreation. None of this is new. What constitutes Frazier's novelty and
advance—the inner mechanism of his social machine for living—
is the particular means by which to achieve what are, after all,
traditional ends.

What I am referring to is Frazier's *idée fixe*, "the control of human behavior," and the degree to which he has set about programming people to lead what he calls (in terminology parodied mercilessly in the literature of dystopia) "a full and satisfying life." Contemptuous of history and metaphysics alike, Frazier has no interest in contemplating the meaning of human nature or, as Skinner puts it elsewhere, "man *qua* man."[36] Rather, he proposes the living example of his community as the answer to two behaviorist questions. "What is the best behavior for the individual as far as the group is concerned? And how can the individual be induced to behave that way?" Once again, the human ideal Frazier holds out to us is someone cooperative, concerned for the well-being of others, docile in manner if not in mind, and so on. But it is the question of "inducement" that signifies a departure—and that has caused such a furor among readers.

For what Frazier has done at Walden Two is begun to raise a generation that has gone through the Air Crib (a mechanical baby tender related to the famous "Skinner box") and been shaped by a program of "positive reinforcement" designed to reward good behavior and discourage bad. What Plato, More and the rest left to the vagaries of moral development and peer pressure, the planner of Walden Two has turned into science. The process begins at birth. Infants are raised in perfect environments totally free of frustration or anxiety. Into this clear plastic Eden the realities of the world are gradually introduced in manageable doses: mild pain, small obstacles, programmed discouragement. Under the watchful eye of experts, the infant is then guided to make positive responses to "aversive stimuli" rather than screaming or striking out in rage. A similar course awaits these children when they are finally hatched from their bubble world, as they come more and more to internalize positive responses and learn the powers of self-control; to become persons who can respond to life "affirmatively." Moreoever, through these techniques of conditioning the community can breed out of its system whatever is counterproductive to the "behavioral repertoire" of the whole population. When Frazier responds to a visitor's question about the emotional life of utopia, he makes it clear that there are some feelings which will simply have to go: not "the productive and strengthening emotions—joy and love. But sorrow and hate—and the high-voltage excitements of anger, fear, and rage—

are out of proportion with the needs of modern life, and they're wasteful and dangerous."

At the heart of the book is the question Frazier poses to those uneasy with his program: "Suppose you suddenly found it possible to control the behavior of men as you wished. What would you do?" All that Plato's philosopher-king or More's Utopus or Bellamy's "guardians" ultimately left to hope, Frazier sees within human control. Whereas Le Corbusier offered us new cities for old, the behaviorist goes right to the heart of the matter, to old human nature, and asks us to exchange a long history of self-defeat for a future in which we will be "more productive and successful"—not because of any miracle or change of character, but merely through the intelligent implementation of modern techniques. Frazier promises a "superorganism," a new and improved human product.

As we listen to all of this, we slowly realize another way in which Skinner's book is a departure. For while the founders of older utopias always disappear into the fabric of their creations, at least by the time we as readers get a chance to make our visit, Skinner places his founding father directly before us. Feature by feature he gives us the lay of *his* land. The closest we have come to this is Le Corbusier's *Radiant City*, in whose drawings and prose we are constantly aware of the architect guiding us through his own designs, like an articulate real estate agent intent upon making a sale. This presence is uncannily emphasized, moreover, in the photographs of Le Corbusier bending over the mock-ups of his metropolis. In pictures of what appear to be real buildings the architect's finger will appear, in order to point up some feature or detail of the model. The effect is disconcerting, as if the master builder were some version of Michelangelo's God the Father caught in the act of touching a newborn Adam into life.

Frazier's overbearing presence reminds us of the enormity of every utopian planner's undertaking. For what is the creator of the plan but a rival creator, one who stands in the place of God as he contemplates the work of his hands and declares it to be good? Skinner does not shy away from this identification; he even underscores it in a scene between Frazier and Burris at the novel's thematic climax. From a hill top overlooking the community's cluster of buildings below—a promontory Frazier calls "The Throne"—we are placed in a situation which alludes unmistakably

to both the gospel temptation narratives and to the Grand Inquisitor passage from *The Brothers Karamazov*. Burris speaks first:

> "Just so you don't think you're God," I said hesi-
> tantly, hoping to bring matters out into the open.
> "There's a curious similarity," [Frazier] said.
> I suffered a moment of panic.
> "Rather considerably less control in your case, I
> should imagine," I said, attempting to adopt a casual
> tone.
> "Not at all," he said, looking up. "At least, if we
> can believe the theologians. On the contrary, it's the
> other way round. You may remember that God's
> children are always disappointing Him.
> "I don't say that I'm never disappointed, but I
> imagine I'm rather less frequently so than God. After
> all, look at the world *He* made."

We have gotten used to thinking about utopia as a response
to our own human imperfection, as a way of cleaning up after
ourselves to avoid polluting the future. But here we see the
impulse to build a perfect world in a new light—as an improvement upon God. Having learned from divine mistakes, Frazier-
Skinner will factor out that supposed predisposition toward
evil that Christians call original sin and replace it with an
imprinting for good. He will enable ordinary people to do
routinely and unthinkingly what in the past only the most
virtuous were able to achieve through strenuous acts of choice.
For like the Grand Inquisitor, Frazier has saved the humans in
his charge from doing harm to others and to themselves by carefully withdrawing certain responses from their repertoire and
thus enabling them "freely" to choose the good. He has made a
better creature, and therefore shown himself a better creator,
than God.
    The publication of Skinner's book caused on outcry which,
in his foreword to the second (1976) edition, the author still seems
anxious to allay. We have no reason to doubt the urgency of his
concerns, especially now, at a time almost forty years after the
first appearance of his novel, when the lack of intelligent planning
in every aspect of the environment, as well as the danger of

nuclear self-destruction, make the issue of control a lively one. But for anyone who comes to *Walden Two* from Orwell's *1984*, it is difficult to hear of Frazier's intentionally benign programming of response without also thinking of Winston Smith being taught that two and two make five. Extensive management of human beings makes us wary, especially as we contemplate the carefully regulated Air Crib and its regimen of positive reinforcement. Besides, are we sure that we would want to become Frazier's "superorganism"? Would being programmed for goodness avoid catastrophe or would it be itself catastrophic—an evasion of the same moral process that constitutes our humanity? And while we are objecting, can we agree with Skinner that goodness is finally a matter of social consensus, and therefore entirely relative? For that matter, can anyone "make" us happy?

Walker Percy's response to all these questions is a resounding no. In essay and fiction alike—and especially in his 1971 novel, *Love in the Ruins*, published in the same year as Skinner's *Beyond Freedom and Dignity*—his special delight has been to take the varieties of utopian impulse in the twentieth century, inflate them to their bursting point, and then enjoy the explosion. Percy wants to demonstrate the inevitable breakdown of any scheme for "implementing" human happiness; he wants, that is, to bring utopia into ruin. But this act of destruction is only a preliminary step, a mere clearing of the decks. His real point is to show how it is possible for someone to be happy in an imperfect world, surrounded by the wreckage of dreams about ideal community and among the denizens of the Radiant City that never came to be. Percy wants, in other words, to teach us the pleasure of ruins.

He does this from a traditional Christian position that ultimately locates the problems of society within the human soul and sees their remedy, not primarily in acts of social or political reform, but in the experience of personal conversion. For Percy we can never make a happy new world by fiat; but we can, by God's grace, be born anew. In this emphasis on the inner self he shares a kinship with Zamiatin and Orwell, who emphasize the precious value of interiority in their portrayal of the individual's battle against the collective mind. Yet Percy neither describes a dystopian nightmare nor sees his vocation as a prophet of doom. To be sure, he is the first to admit things are not well with us, and knows that it is the business of the serious writer to say so in no uncertain terms. But there are for him other ways to give warning about our contemporary malaise than through the tactics of fear. And so he uses the weapons of laughter to make utopian solutions seem ridiculous and grotesque; he disarms them through humor.

Percy's comic sense helps us to realize by contrast how sober an affair the literature of utopia has been. Either it bores us with lectures on the happy life or scares us into fear and trembling with forecasts of a global prison camp beyond freedom and dignity. There has been precious little of the smiling we were occasionally permitted in More's original work, for since its jocular beginning the tradition has come to take itself very seriously indeed. This solemnity is understandable given utopia's standard assumption that the world is largely in human hands, for better or for worse. With Percy, however, our existence rests finally in other hands. We may very well bring on catastrophe, or even bring about dramatic improvements, but in the end our lives are not our own— either to damn or to save. There are limits to our control.

In an essay entitled, "A Novel About the End of the World," which preceded the publication of *Love in the Ruins* by a few years and serves as a kind of prospectus for it, Percy identifies the hero of post-modern fiction as "a man who has forgotten his bad memories and conquered his present ills and who finds himself in the victorious Secular City. His only problem now is to keep from blowing his brains out."[37] He asks us, in other words, to imagine Julian West in the year 2010 or Professor Burris after a decade or so at Walden Two—but not as happy citizens of a utopia which has provided for their every physical want. No, he asks us to think of them instead as persons inexplicably miserable in the Radiant City. With stomachs full and work no longer a burden, with peace and general prosperity, there seem at last to be no real negatives to negate—except, possibly, for the big one. Despair. How do we keep from blowing our brains out?

The protagonist of Percy's third novel is just such a man. He is in the middle of his life, in decent though much abused health, with more money than he knows what to do with and a position of prominence and respect within his community. He lives in a place called "Paradise Estates," enriched by every comfort and convenience the latter part of the twentieth century can afford. And yet he keeps on slashing his wrists, passing out drunk, and checking himself into mental wards.

Percy names his protagonist "Thomas More." Like his illustrious collateral ancestor, he too is a Catholic, a sort of public servant, at odds with the age in which he lives and capable of imagining a better world altogether. But unlike that "great soul, the dearest best noblest of Englishmen," he is a *bad* Catholic whose wife has left him and whose child has died, a scientist rather than a saint, and a martyr to nothing more than his own malaise. *Doctor* Thomas More is a physician who cannot heal himself, who is torn apart by the contrary impulses that rage within him, having at once a very orthodox religious sensibility ("I believe in the Holy Catholic Apostolic and Roman Church, in God the Father, in the election of the Jews, in Jesus Christ His Son our Lord . . .") *and* the countervailing ambition of a psychiatrist on the make who wants the Nobel Prize for a technique of behavior modification that (he feels certain) will change the world for the "better." Between one More and the other is a great gulf fixed:

> Why can't I follow More's example, love myself less,
> God and my fellowman more, and leave whiskey and
> women alone? Sir Thomas More was merry in life and
> death and he loved and was loved by everyone, even
> his executioner, with whom he cracked jokes. By con-
> trast I am possessed by terror and desire and live a
> solitary life. My life is a longing, longings for women,
> for the Nobel Prize, for the hot bosky bite of bourbon
> whiskey, and other heart-wrenching longings that have
> no name. Sir Thomas was right, of course, and I am
> wrong. But on the other hand these are peculiar
> times. . . .

For More the times are reaching a pitch of frenzy so apocalyptic that he feels himself "near the end of the world" and on the threshold of Armageddon. The war within his members is merely an individual manifestation of conflicts that threaten to split his entire society asunder—a society which we recognize after only a few satiric strokes to be a souped-up version of our own late 1960's. Percy sets his novel in the South, on the Gulf, and at some unspecified Fourth of July in the future; say, in the year 1984, or perhaps even closer to Bellamy's turn of the millenium. "Wickedness flourishes in high places," observes the prophetic doctor, as the war in South Ecuador rumbles on and the

American microcosm that More opens up to us begins to pull
apart in opposite directions. He alone has no fixed place, wandering freely from one social group to another; nowhere at home, he
is in some sense welcome everywhere. Thus his dislocation
enables him to see an entire social panorama from a perspective
of extraordinary mobility, even though it makes him a displaced
person in whatever camp he enters.

On the political right, and concentrated in the unnamed town
where the doctor keeps his office, we find "a refuge for all manner
of conservative folks, graduates of Bob Jones University, retired
Air Force colonels, passed-over Navy commanders, ex-Washington,
D.C. policemen, patriotic chiropractors, two officials of the
National Rifle Association, and six conservative proctologists."
The townspeople who consult More for their psychiatric problems
bring him the ailments that seem peculiarly to afflict the Right:
unreasonable rages, delusions of conspiracy, large bowel com-
plaints. They are all fighting mad.

On the other side of the political spectrum (and on the other
side of town) there is the "Fedville" complex where More has
been a professor of psychiatric medicine as well as an inmate of a
psychiatric ward. Fedville is the monolithic, federally-sponsored
center of America's self-help industry. It is the home of medical
research, NASA, the Behavioral Institute, the Love Clinic, and the
Geriatric Rehabilitation Center (known more familiarly as "Gerry
Rehab"). This is where the spirit of B.F. Skinner, along with
those of Masters and Johnson, increase and multiply their reme-
dies. Fedville folk lean to the Left and suffer its sinister com-
plaints: sexual impotence, morning terrors, feelings of abstraction
and ennui, crippling anxieties of every kind. It is against these
problems that the wheels of the behaviorists spin night and day in
their pursuit of a happier adjustment.

Standing geographically between Fedville and the town, as
well as bridging the ideological gap that stretches between them, is
Paradise Estates, the upper-middle-class enclave where Dr. More
lives. There we find strange and unnatural alliances, as conservative proctologists and liberal behaviorists amicably agree to disagree, joined as they are by a common bourgeois life style that
seems effectively to ignore (if not overcome) real differences of
belief. Virtually indistinguishable, they play golf, drink toddies,
and ride about on miniature tractor-mowers—oblivious to the

vines that are sprouting everywhere and to the social unrest that
those vines portend.

Behind the shopping malls that ring the country club, there
stretches the vast Honey Island Swamp. It is home not only to the
community's poorest blacks, but to a group of downwardly
mobile hippies living out a pharmacologically maintained utopian
escape in a grassy "cloud palace". But included in the swamp's
demographic hodge-podge there are far stranger types, misfits
drawn from every fringe of American culture:

> Bantu guerillas, dropouts from Tulane and Vanderbilt,
> M.I.T. and Loyola; draft dodgers, deserters from the
> Swedish Army, psychopaths and pederasts from
> Memphis and Mobile whose practices were not even to
> be tolerated in New Orleans; anti-papal Catholics, mal-
> contented Methodists, ESPers, UFOers, ex-Ayn Randers,
> Chocktaw Zionists who have returned to their ancestral
> hunting grounds. . . .

Honey Island is Haight Ashbury in 1968, a place to which people
have come to pursue the unfettered dream of a better life—or
simply to take refuge when they have no place else to go. In all
its diversity and fragmentation it is located "nowhere" in mainstream American life, standing on its own as an ill-defined but
nonetheless alternate world.

Over the course of the novel, as Dr. More describes these
adjacent but self-isolating "subdivisions" within the larger community, he is in fact giving us Walker Percy's satirical portrait of
our culture. We see America as it might be glimpsed in a Fun
House mirror: a cheerful grotesque which, however amusing,
flatters no one it reflects. Although at times absurdly reductive
in its distortion and exaggeration, it is a looking glass that offers
us an image of ourselves—if not a "true" likeness, then at the very
least a telling one. For what we find are a host of American types
(the Good Old Boy, the Super Negro, the Dumb Blonde, the
"Advanced" Scientist), all blindly pursuing their notions of the
good life as there swirls about them a chaos of brand names, TV
lore, and modern opinion. Because the novel's satiric thrust is
conveyed by a persona as winsome and vulnerable as Dr. More—
or because Percy feels an affection for what he also disdains—the

negating of the negative in this particular portrayal of human existence lacks the self-righteousness of most utopian literature, as well the anti-utopian's sense of horror and revulsion. We are led to acknowledge this thing of darkness to be our own: a silly, frantic world, to be sure, but one ripe for redeeming. And so, having established that we are at a moment of crisis, a time near the end of the world when the center does not hold and the apocalyptic axe is laid to the root, Dr. More presents a solution for his troubled microcosm of America. As an unknown sniper fires his bullets and a volatile society threatens to boil over on the anniversary of its independence, we are treated to yet another version of utopia's dream. A brave new world is in the offing.

Most utopian thinkers begin their imaginative act of renovation with an analysis of the political and economic realities bedeviling the "old" world, in the course of which they give some rationale for massive social change. Yet Percy's Dr. More makes another kind of diagnosis entirely. He is not interested in class struggle, or the institution of racism, or the impact of astroturf on a putting-green economy. No, he is obsessed by spiritual warfare, a schizophrenia within the modern soul that gradually has undermined the psychic (and social) foundations of the West since the Renaissance, "since the famous philosopher Descartes ripped body loose from mind and turned the very soul into a ghost that haunts its own house."

The center does not hold because there is a central division within ourselves: a split between body and mind, head and heart. Either we are oppressed by the beast within us—angry, aggressive, libidinal, destructive—or we are strung out in angelic abstraction, with its vague anxieties and disembodied longings. Hence the ailments that pester the Right and the Left, the town and Fedville, as well as Dr. More's own mood swings between "night-time exaltations," when the beast roams free, and "morning terrors," when the dark angel of anxiety is in charge. In this light we can also understand the social violence that builds steadily as the narrative unfolds, threatening an explosion of catastrophic proportions and (as the subtitle reads) the "end of the world."

Love in the Ruins is not a work of despair whose nightmare has come true, yet it portrays the dire consequences of modernity on both individual and community as a sickness introduced into

Western culture during the hopeful same period of renaissance
that spawned utopia. In his "Oration on the Dignity of Man"
Pico encouraged us to believe that we could all become angels
if we worked hard enough at not being beasts. What Percy shows
us, on the other hand, is a world oscillating madly between the
two extremes, thereby losing touch with the incarnate union of
spirit and flesh that *is* human nature. What we see destroyed, in
other words, is ourselves—not at the hands of party or despot or
plan, but as the slowly lethal result of "enlightened" values. As
one character confesses, in the midst of a nervous breakdown that
actually reveals his essential sanity, "I am surrounded by the
corpses of souls. We live in a city of the dead." His observation
carries the real burden of *Love in the Ruins*, although it will be
brought home through laughter rather than tears.

Within the array of social options the novel presents, we are
shown two ways that people have dealt with psychic fissure, each
an unheralded utopian remedy. One is a classic example of retreat
to a would-be island paradise, a Mexican arts and crafts community
off the Yucatan, where the hard realities of twentieth-century life
have all been "transcended." It is where More's wife escapes after
the death of her child and breakdown of her marriage. An
example of "angelic" utopianism at its most muddle-headed and
fantasy-ridden, it offers a "true community life stripped of its
technological dross . . . simple meetings and greetings, spiritual
communications, the touch of a hand, etcetera, etcetera."

The other model for coping is represented by the massive
Fedville complex, and by two of its institutions in particular: the
Love Clinic and the Geriatric Rehabilitation Center. These are the
places where science, technology, and the most advanced (and
value-free) psychological theory undertake the task of human
happiness. The sexually dysfunctional are trained like rats to go
through all the right erotic emotions in order "to achieve satis-
factory response." Meanwhile, criminals are straightened out in
the Skinner box, which can "condition away the contradictions"
between desire and fulfillment to eradicate every trace of inhib-
iting guilt. Fedville is also where the elderly are brought into line,
for it is they who have turned out to be most resistant to the "new
and happy life" America has invented for them. The situation, in
fact, has reached epidemic proportions.

> Old folks from Tampa to Tucson are treated for the
> blues and boredoms of old age. . . . Though their every
> need is filled, every recreation provided, every sort of
> hobby encouraged, nevertheless many grow despondent
> in their happiness, sit slack and empty-eyed at shuffle-
> board and ceramic oven. Fishing poles fall from
> tanned and healthy hands. Golf clubs rust. *Reader's
> Digests* go unread. Many old folks pine away and even
> die from unknown causes like victims of a voodoo
> curse. Here in Gerry Rehab, these sad oldsters are en-
> couraged to develop their 'creative and artistic poten-
> tial.' Yet mysterious deaths, and suicides too, continue
> to mount.

Percy takes the infantilization of elderly people already in practice
"from Tampa to Tucson"—the familiar palaver of social workers
("creative and artistic potential"), the routine distractions suggested by *Modern Maturity*, and the whole "retirement industry"—and makes them seem as bizarre as a voodoo curse. He
makes us aware of how degrading the well-meaning but oppressive
custody of the old can be, simply by using phrases from common
usage and expressed *ad seriatum* in a relentlessly passive voice:
"their every need is filled, every recreation provided, every sort of
hobby encouraged." We are shown how it is possible, and with
the best of intentions, to kill with kindness.

What we also realize as the novel moves along is that Gerry
Rehab is a spoof of Walden Two. For it turns out that sufferers
from "St. Petersburg blues" are placed in room-sized Skinner
boxes in which they are given full access to pottery wheels,
putting greens, ceramic ovens, and square dance therapists: the
ingredients for a life of happy retirement. Those who bring themselves to enjoy these pastimes are "encouraged" by tiny pleasant
shocks of electric current; those who respond negatively by
breaking their pottery or kicking their dance therapist, on the
other hand, receive painful ones. At the end of this period of
conditioning, those who respond well are sent back to their senior
settlements; those who do not are shipped off to the "Happy
Isles of Georgia," a federal euthanasia center where they are
conditioned further and eventually choose their own deaths. Like
Zamiatin's D-503 petitioning the authorities for the Great Opera-

tion, they are induced to pull the Happy Isles Switch and thus "voluntarily" end their misery.

Dr. More's personal response to the prevailing malaise is to invent a mechanical device both to diagnose and to solve the human predicament. In the course of his research, he has discovered a way to calculate human suffering, to "observe, measure and verify" the degree to which a person has lost his or her self. He names the gadget "More's Qualitative Quantitative Ontological Lapsometer" because it measures the fall from human wholeness. The next step (which he is certain will bring him the Nobel Prize) promises to take him beyond diagnosis and into treatment—and with it, reentry into the lost world that every utopia has hoped to reconstruct. "Suppose ---! Suppose I could hit on the right dosage and weld the broken self whole! What if man could reenter paradise, so to speak, and live there both as man and spirit, whole and intact man-spirit, as solid flesh as a speckled trout, a dappled thing, yet aware of itself as a self!"

Frazier's question in *Walden Two* comes immediately to mind: "Suppose you suddenly found it possible to control the behavior of men as you wished. What would you do?" More's answer is clear. He would reverse the Fall, reintegrate humanity, and give people the wherewithal to be happy—not by changing the structures of their environment and conditioning, but by instantly and effortlessly renewing their minds for them. What he does not seem to realize, however, is the fault line of contradiction that runs right through the middle of his dream. For what he proposes as the remedy for a spiritual problem—identified for us as "the broken self"—is to be brought about by something like "modern techniques," by a gadget which affords us simply another version of Fedville conditioning. He will reverse the Fall through an application of scientific method; he will make a new Adam, and rewrite Genesis on his own terms. We think of Le Corbusier's promise in *The Radiant City* to "dispel the miasma of anxiety now darkening our lives." With More we again see the impulse that may be inherent in all utopian imagining, although especially powerful when unrestrained by some notion of human limitation and divine transcendence. Invariably utopia wants to start up all over again, do it right for the last time, getting better results out of the world than God has seen fit (or been able) to achieve.

But even as we catch Dr. More wild-eyed in the act of utopian
imagining, Percy makes us realize the mania which is lodged within
his excitement. The poor sick fool stands at the center of his own
whirlwind. For the same More who would weld the broken self
whole has been ripped loose from himself, and his solution to
human brokenness is itself an example of the very problem he
would solve. He does not have it of himself to help himself; the
planner is at a loss. That More's impulse is not only pathetic but
diabolical is suggested by a character who mysteriously appears:
More's outlandish shadow self, Art Immelman, who is eager to
give Dr. More the potential (in the jargon of this hi-tech Willy
Loman) "to utilize technique that maximizes and unites hardware
and software opportunities." What this offer amounts to is the
technology needed to realize More's dream: to turn the lapsometer
into a device for treatment and thereby to effect any change in
human behavior he sees fit to make. In this way Immelman plays
Mephistofeles to More's Faust, giving him not only the power to
refashion humanity, but the chance "of being like a God in
freedom and omniscience." And so, just as Zamiatin, Orwell
and Skinner all return the reader to Dostoevsky's Grand Inquisitor
by way of setting their works in what amounts to a religious
context, so Percy's novel circles back to a still more foundational
text—to Genesis 3—and with that story brings us face to face with
Satan's original offer that we should be "as gods."

No one, however, reenters the Garden. While Percy's plot
defies summarization, it is sufficient to say that the catastrophe
toward which the narrative seemed to be driving us never occurs,
nor, thanks to a miraculous intervention by *Saint* Thomas More,
does Immelman get to claim the Doctor's soul. In an epilogue
set five years after the main action of the novel, Percy returns us
to a world still waiting to be reformed by cataclysm, political
revolution, or flights of utopian fantasy. At most, we can say
that the ruins of Western civilization have been reorganized. The
formerly disenfranchised blacks now lord it over the newly impoverished whites, not as a result of the Bantu uprising (which
never came to pass), but due to a fluke in real estate values—an
old fashioned capitalist reversal of fortunes! Their squatters'
refuge in Honey Island Swamp turned out to be an oil field whose
flood of black gold has carried them from the old slave quarters
on the edge of the swamp to the stately homes of Paradise Estates.

There they sit at the top of a social structure which is identical to
its predecessor save for a superficial change in color.

What is genuinely different, however, is Dr. More. To be sure,
he retains his old weakness for bourbon, his penchant for sexual
dalliance, and his determination to redeem the twentieth century
with his psycho-spiritual device: "I still believe my lapsometer
can save the world—if I can get it right. For the world is broken,
sundered, busted down the middle, self ripped from self and man
pasted back together as mythical monster, half angel, half beast,
but no man. Even now I can diagnose and shall one day cure:
cure the new plague, the modern Black Death. . . ." Yet despite
the persistence of this delusion, he is not the same man we knew
five years before. No, he has married again, fathered two children,
contented himself with a modest medical practice and no Nobel
Prize; in short, More has accepted his finitude with grace. Percy
presents him at the beginning of the epilogue as some postlapsarian Adam, happily making do outside the precincts of Eden—
a southern Candide hoeing collards in his garden. In the absence
of utopia (or when the fever for it passes), *il faut cultiver notre
jardin.*

What has happened? More comes to see brokenness and incompletion as aspects of our fallen human nature, which can
never be eradicated by modern techniques without doing serious
damage to our essential humanity. He accepts our sense of dislocation in the world as a sheer fact of existence, not necessarily
as something to be cured, and comes to discover the dignity in our
situation. If we are in some deep sense out of place wherever
we live, we are nonetheless "sovereign wanderers" and "lordly
exiles"—creatures who belong here only temporarily, but who
receive our sovereignty and lordship from the divine kingdom
which Flannery O'Connor called our "true country." In the
world but not of it, we are citizens of earth whose conversation,
finally, is in heaven.

At the end of the novel Dr. More is on his way to exchanging
utopian hopes for St. Paul's "earnest expectation" of a kingdom
not of this world. He has become a watchman at the gates, expecting a further revelation in God's own time—a time which (who
knows?) may be our own. As More reflects in a kind of millennial
reverie that contrasts so markedly with his old forebodings, "This
morning, hauling up a great unclassified beast of a fish, I thought

of Christ coming again at the end of the world and how it is that
in every age there is the temptation to see signs of the end and
that, even knowing this, there is nevertheless some reason, what
with the spirit of the new age being the spirit of watching and
waiting, to believe that—"

This realization of transcendence is not some private *tao*,
or an inner path to be trod alone; it is an understanding handed
down by tradition and within a community, to be shared with
other "workers and waiters and watchers." Where Percy has his
protagonist find his place, along with a comically motley crew of
other exiles and wanderers, is in the little chapel that abuts the
old slave quarters where More now lives. It is a flock shepherded
by Father Rinaldo Smith, who has emerged from the "city of the
dead" to serve a Catholic remnant no less bizarre in its way than
the denizens of Honey Island Swamp. Whereas the main body of
the novel unfolds around the July Fourth holiday, the epilogue
brings us to Christmas Eve and an image of genuine (if incomplete) human community. This is the best of all the possible
worlds which *Love in the Ruins* has to offer us. In a post-
Christian era, with Bantu religion now in effect the established
faith, those who keep alive the biblical religions find themselves
thrown together by a happy coincidence of sacred time into the
same ramshackle place:

> The Jews are leaving—it is their Sabbath. The Protes-
> tants are singing at the end of their service. Catholics
> are lined up for confession, preparing for midnight
> mass. We have no ecumenical movement. No minutes
> of the previous meeting are kept. The services overlap.
> Jews wait for the Lord, Protestants sing hymns to him,
> Catholics say mass and eat him.

It is in this setting of imperfect reconciliation that More goes to
confession for the first time in years and thereby restores himself
to communion with his church. On the feast of the Incarnation,
in the midst of a celebration of God's greatest gift—"whole and
intact man-spirit"—he finds himself part of the Body of Christ.
It is neither as a genius nor a savior that he stands before the
reader, but only as an ordinary sinner, redeemed from the prin-
cipalities and powers that vex the modern world and able to live
in its ruins with something very much like joy.

Happiness has the last word in *Love in the Ruins*, as Walker
Percy brings together the broken pieces of this incoherent social
landscape into an image of living hope. In the penultimate chapter
of the epilogue Dr. More is met after mass by a black man who is
running for Congress with the support of various constituencies—
bohemian swamp people, liberals, "peckerwoods"—all formerly at
violent odds with one another. He comes to More looking for
help with the Catholic vote. The doctor at first is skeptical, then
amused, but no longer is driven by the old messianic fantasies
("I can save you, America!") to do it all himself. In the end,
moreover, he decides to throw in his lot with this unlikely coali-
tion foolish (or faithful) enough to try working within the system.
With his children's shouts still ringing in his ears (" 'Hurray for
Jesus Christ!' they cry. 'Hurray for the United States!' "), he is,
like the character "Thomas More" in *Utopia*, willing to hope for
more than he ever expects to see.

But this measure of political engagement as Catholic vote-
getter for a black man's congressional seat is not where Percy
leaves either his hero or the reader who has followed his development from visionary know-it-all to "worker and waiter and
watcher." In its concluding scene the novel brings us home to the
slave quarters, in the wee hours of Christmas morning, where More
and his second wife climb into the six hundred dollar king-size bed
he has bought her as a present.

> To bed we go for a long winter's nap, twined about each
> other as the ivy twineth, not under a bus or in a car or
> on the floor or any such humbug as marked the past
> peculiar years of Christendom, but at home in bed where
> all good folk belong.

This is how More's story draws to a close, with a picture of
happy people in an unhappy world, as the ivy twines around
domestic bliss where once the vines sprouted their forecasts of
doom. Visions of utopia, hopes of reentering paradise, delusions
of grandeur: all have now given way to a far more modest proposal. And so we see More after his communion, both a member
of a community awaiting the fuller revelation of the kingdom of
God *and* a husband comfortably tucked into bed in the arms of
his wife. The novel's reply to his earlier utopian longings—and its
presumed prescription to the reader for finding love in the ruins—

is a humble version of *Kinder, Kirche, Kuche*, left open to whatever God and God alone will give.

* * *

Love in the Ruins presents us with the explicitly Christian
critique of utopian imagining we have lacked ever since Sir
Thomas More's *The Best State of a Commonwealth* started us
dreaming in concrete terms. Percy does not carry on the tradition
by having his hero build a new community in the Honey Island
Swamp, nor allows himself to fantasize what the "spirit of
the new age" would mean for political institutions or the distribution of wealth. Instead, he shows us folk beginning to work
within the "same old funny fouled-up" system—and going to
church. The Christmas Eve confusion of Jews and Christians
milling about the former slave chapel is the closest Percy comes
to ideal community. Totally peripheral to the center of culture,
it is a refuge from society rather than an image of its renewal.

In this preference for the religious "counter-culture," quietly
bearing its witness in the midst of spiritually alien territory,
Percy emerges as a twentieth-century soul mate of St. Augustine
(although blessed with a sense of humor not readily found in the
Bishop of Hippo). As his "Rome" seems to be falling into ruin—
"Is it that God at last has removed his blessing from the U.S.A.?"
More asks on the novel's first page—he grinds his axe on behalf
of the City of God against the pagans and encourages his pilgrim
reader along the way. With a strong conviction about human
limitation that puts him at odds with utopia's faith in the great
leap forward, he has a nose for the *libido dominandi* that often
lurks within grand schemes for improvement. Believing with
Augustine that we are creatures who restlessly live in longing,
whose needs can never be satisfied by the "city of this world,"
Percy celebrates our incompletion, aware that it keeps us looking
beyond ourselves and hungry for God. Where he and Augustine
part company, however, is in Percy's esteem for the warm,
dappled, fleshly aspects of human existence, which have been as
much neglected by Christian theology as by utopia. Thus, while
the "sovereign wanderer" of *Love in the Ruins* finds himself a
wayfarer on earth, marching toward a kingdom that is not of
this world, he is also a lusty husband about to make love to his

wife. He is not simply passing through a world that is (truly) not his home; he has learned to enjoy the temporary stay.

In the high value he places on the fleshly and finite, Percy is also at one with writers like Zamiatin and Orwell who do not otherwise share his theological convictions. Allied with them in a common fear of what modernity is capable of doing to us for our own good, he shares their suspicion of disembodied reason as well as their awareness of the diabolical possibilities of intellectuals in power. While the city of this world may become increasingly a "city of the dead," where surviving human beings walk among the corpses of souls as members of an endangered species, the remedy for the problem lies neither in revolutionary solution nor comprehensive plan. It lies rather in what individuals find for themselves in moments of passion and affection, in dreams of a "golden country" which strengthen us to live in that Age of Iron which is all that history has ever allowed us.

Where Percy diverges from these other opponents of utopia is in his lack of despair over the world's prospects, however pessimistic he may be about majority rule or the sway of experts. Unlike Orwell, for instance, whose *1984* shows our century wholly annexed by totalitarian nightmare, he always has the church as a community of resistance, a witness to sanity. There is something against which hell cannot prevail. For Percy it is as impossible to imagine humanity utterly abandoned by God as it is to imagine us made perfect by our own efforts. He refuses to admit the extinction of grace, insisting on the contrary that we remember the surprise of the transcendent intruding its way into our experience when least expected, and under the worst conditions. To allow that there is no hope is to forget that there is a limit not only to our goodness, but also to our evil. History shows us that people under the most annihilating of conditions and at untold cost of suffering have been able to withstand the apparently overwhelming horror of battlefield or concentration camp or gulag by "watching and waiting and thinking and working"—by holding on to their humanity. The cautionary tales of the anti-utopians, therefore, tell a lie which immobilizes with fear rather than energizes for prevention. They have betrayed the truth there has never been a ruin so awful that people have not loved in the midst of it.

Percy deflates both utopian optimism and anti-utopian doom.

In their different ways they are too grand, too self-important for
the humbler prescription that he offers through his apostle of
common sense, Fr. Smith. Confronted by More's pretenses, the
arrogance that lingers from his earlier heroic mode, the priest
delivers what I imagine to be Percy's own rebuttal of utopia:

> There are other things we must think about: like doing
> our jobs, you being a better doctor, I being a better
> priest, showing a bit of ordinary kindness to people,
> particularly our own families—unkindness to those close
> to us is such a pitiful thing—doing what we can for our
> poor country—things which, please forgive me, some-
> times seem more important than dwelling on a few
> middle-aged daydreams.

This injunction to common decency, which accepts the world as
it is and urges us to make the best of it, serves as a sensible put-
down to any number of dreams. Eat Christ, drink his blood, and
be merry in bed—this is what More discovers in the end. It seems
enough to get one's own little house in order and pray the kingdom come. And yet, for all the Christian realism and good
common sense that shine through Percy's pages, I find myself
coming from this engaging novel *almost*, but not quite, persuaded.
It is strange to admit this reservation when, by temperament and
experience, the path finally taken by Dr. More is the one most
immediately and personally compelling.

It is difficult to dispute the sensible truth of doing what we
can with a bad thing and with as much joy as possible. But
perhaps what I miss in the novel's antidote to prophetic delusion
is one particular aspect of the genuine prophetic voice, one which
will speak to the *material* issues of its world. The literature of
utopia has taught me, after all, to listen for its witness, its call to
reexamine what we mistakenly take for granted as necessity, to
ask us to imagine how society might be made more just. We have
heard this voice in the outraged cry of Raphael Hythloday as he
contemplates the destruction of England's poor, in the deep concern of Edward Bellamy for a more equitable distribution of
wealth, and in Le Corbusier's manifesto of the right of ordinary
people to sunlight and air and a healthy place to life. I have
already taken each of these to task for one thing or another, and

missed in every case the attention to individual reality that Percy celebrates so appealingly. And yet I find it impossible to dismiss the preoccupations they share: the way the life of the individual is tied to social conditions, how people earn their living, the political and economic structures that deform us rather than giving us a chance to flourish.

Like Percy's other heroes, all anxious sons of the comfortable middle class, More is free to pursue his neuroses (or his religious quest) unhampered by worry over the material needs of the morrow. While suspicious of utopian schemes, Percy has other negatives to negate than those that have traditionally been a preoccupation. Writing for an American middle-class audience with its physical welfare largely achieved, he concerns himself instead with the distortions of the modern spirit rather than with the needs of its flesh—with angelism and bestialism rather than bad housing. His work is genuinely prophetic, cutting through the false gods of our century and then, in the imaginative clearing opened up by satire, offering a Christian image of the happy life. It is also the one most likely to succeed in what More calls "these dread latter days of the violent beloved U.S.A. and of the Christ-forgetting Christ-haunted death-dealing Western world."

By choosing as his protagonist a character named Thomas More, Percy inevitably leads us to see the contrast between his Catholic predecessor's breadth of vision and his own more narrowly existential concerns. To be sure, Percy describes a social world in great detail, but in the end he attends seriously only to the religious transformation of a single man, as if the corporate sphere were past helping and, in any case, of secondary concern. Unlike *Utopia*, his novel leaves us with a happy ending that pulls up the covers and turns out the lights—not the unresolved burden of the real Thomas More's work, which (as a history of its reading abundantly shows) turns us back into the world with the desire to change it. Perhaps the night is too far spent, our age too ravaged by one kind of revolution or another, to give way to optimism about society as it might be or to imagine concretely how "our poor country" might be made less of a mess. In any event, it must be noted that the Thomas More who is explicitly recalled in *Love in the Ruins* is, significantly, *not* the young man on the brink of service to his prince and ready to do what he could for the commonwealth—not the author of *Utopia* at all.

Instead, Percy's novel only remembers the martyr standing at
the dead end of his political career, merrily jesting with his
executioner just before the axe did its work. That "great soul,"
as the Doctor calls him, could laugh in the ruins of all his earnest
dreams precisely because his hopes were never placed in utopia
at all, let alone in England. The way he kept his sanity was by
living in terms of another kingdom, one not of this world.

But what about *this* world? In our own time we have come
to see a dramatic polarization between Christians who value the
legacy of utopian thought and those who do not. There is a
division between those who see the liberation of social and
economic injustice as the contemporary mandate of the church
and those who view this secular emphasis as an adulteration of the
gospel's fundamentally spiritual message. It is interesting to
speculate in which of these camps Thomas More would stand
today, exposed (as Walker Percy has been) to the politicization
of utopian ideals for better and, quite decidedly, for worse.
Certainly it took only a few years after the 1516 publication of
his book for More's own position on the human prospect to
harden, as the rise of Protestantism and its myriad demands for
reform—some of them even bolstered by Hythloday's arguments
on the virtues of communism!—made his playful reinvention of
the world seem a folly to be regretted. In his Tower cell, awaiting
the chopping block, *Utopia* might very well have been an unintended sin to confess; it would not, in any case, have remained
a source of hope.

This does not mean, however, that its legacy need be repudi-
ated by us, or that we should accept as hard and fast the line that
has been drawn between the corporate concerns of liberation
theology and an emphasis on individual spiritual transformation.
Indeed, the division into warring camps is precisely the schizophrenia of beast and angel that has resulted in what Percy speaks
of as "no man": in the loss of that embodied spirit which it is the
peculiar mystery of incarnational religion to reveal. A Christian
who takes utopia seriously, therefore, will neither be seduced by
false earthly promises or be content with "religious" experience,
but instead will take the ideal commonwealth *as an ideal*, and one
which God has enabled us to imagine, if never fully to achieve.
Thus, while we acknowledge our perfection to lie beyond us, we
also know we have been given the ability to envision justice,

together with the power and resolve to change social structures on behalf of the common good. Of course to be a brother's keeper is a very dangerous business, as the history of utopian literature and actual experimentation has shown. Nonetheless, it is a risk we are bound to take as we acknowledge ourselves to be members incorporate of political (as well as mystical) bodies, of communities for whose wellbeing God holds us responsible. Like the kingdom for which we have been taught to pray, utopia may be an unknown entity we are called to press toward if never to find. It may be a "nowhere" forever standing beyond our reach, whose sheer unattainability keeps us constantly reaching out for more. Perhaps better understood as a dynamic rather than a design, utopia's best gift is to keep us actively hoping.

NOTES

1. I could not have written this book without the magisterial work of Frank and Fritzie Manuel; it is a pleasure for me to acknowledge their graceful erudition. *Utopian Thought in the Western World* (Cambridge, MA: Harvard University Press, 1979) provides the depth and background upon which my own study draws, even though its focus is upon intellectual history rather than on the theological implications of particular utopian schemes.

2. The translation of Tillich's "Critique and Justification of Utopia" (first published in 1951 as *"Kultur and Rechtfertigung der Utopie"*) is from Frank Manuel's *Utopias and Utopian Thought* (Boston: Houghton Mifflin Co., 1965), pp. 296-309.

3. *Hesiod*, ed. Richard Lattimore (Ann Arbor, MI: University of Michigan Press, 1959), pp. 31-33.

4. See Robert C. Elliott's chapter, "Saturnalia, Satire and Utopia," in *The Shape of Utopia* (Chicago: University of Chicago Press, 1970). Elliott says of the relationship between satire and utopia, "The two modes are formally joined in More's eponymous work, and indeed the very notion of utopia necessarily entails a negative appraisal of present conditions. Satire and utopia are not really separable, the one a critique of the real world in the name of something better, the other a hopeful construct of a world that might be" (p. 24).

5. For beliefs about the earthly paradise, including an account of Columbus's "discovery," see Manuel, *Utopian Thought*, pp. 33-63.

6. Norman Cohn, *The Pursuit of the Millennium* (New York: Oxford University Press, 1970), pp. 19-36.

7. *The Divine Institutes*, trans. Sister Mary Frances McDonald (Washington, DC: Catholic University of America Press, 1964), p. 531.

8. Wolfgang Braunfels, "The St. Gall Utopia," in *Monasteries of Western Europe* (Princeton, NJ: Princeton University Press, 1972), pp. 1-10.

9. *Phaedrus and Letters VII and VIII*, trans. Walter Hamilton (Harmondsworth, Middlesex: Penguin, 1973), p. 114.

10. *The Republic of Plato*, trans. Francis M. Cornford (New York: Oxford University Press, 1963), p. 209.

11. The Manuels give an excellent sense of utopia's intellectual history from Plato to More in their chapter, "The Great Transmission," pp. 93-114.

12. The English text of Pico's "Oration," edited, translated, and introduced by Arturo Fallico and Herman Shapiro, is found in volume 1 of *Renaissance Philosophy* (New York: Modern Library, 1967). For a good introduction see Paul O. Kristeller et al., *Renaissance Philosophy of Man*, (Chicago: University of Chicago Press, 1948), pp. 215-222.

13. For a facsimile text of More's *Life of John Picus* see *The English Works of Thomas More*, ed. W.E. Campbell, vol. 1 (London: Eyre and Spottiswoode, 1931). A helpful discussion of the work and its connection to More's own development is found in Alastair Fox, *Thomas More, History and Providence* (Oxford: Basil Blackwell, 1982), pp. 27-35.

14. My reconstruction of how More came to write Utopia is based on J. H. Hexter's in his splendid introduction to vol. 4 of *The Complete Works of Thomas More* (New Haven: Yale University Press, 1965), especially pp. xxvii-xlv.

15. Cited by Hexter, ibid., p. xxxiii.

16. In *More's Utopia, The Biography of an Idea* (Princeton: Princeton University Press, 1952), J. H. Hexter describes the author's situation at the time of his return to England, pp. 11-29. He also gives an excellent account of the issues involved in Book I's discussion of the philosopher's service to the state (pp. 99-155), as well as an astute appraisal of More's final decision to enter the Royal Council.

17. Stephen Greenblatt in *Renaissance Self-Fashioning, From More to Shakespeare* (Chicago: University of Chicago Press, 1980), pp. 49f, is perceptive on the role of shame in Utopia. See also his discussion of "psychological remodeling," pp. 39f.

18. For the degree to which More throws Hythloday's reliability into doubt, see R. A. Sylvester's essay in *Essential Articles for the Study of Thomas More*, ed. R. S. Sylvester and G. P. Marc'hadour (Hamden, CT: Archon Books, 1977), pp. 390-411.

19. R. S. Chambers in *Thomas More* (London: Jonathan Cape, 1935), p. 128, makes what has come to be the classic formulation of the comparison between Utopia and Christendom by contrasting the good behavior of those who have only reason to guide them with the appalling barbarity of a Europe which has not only reason, but revelation as well: "The underlying thought of Utopia always is, With nothing to guide them, the Utopians do this; and yet we Christian Englishmen, we Christian Europeans. . . !" See also Elliott, pp. 25-49.

20. More to Erasmus, circa 4 December 1516, in *St. Thomas More: Selected Letters*, ed. Elizabeth Frances Rogers (New Haven: Yale University Press, 1961), p. 85.

21. Edward Bellamy, "How I Came to Write 'Looking Backward,' " *The Nationalist* 1 (May 1889): 1-4. It is cited by John L. Thomas in his superb introduction to the Belknap Press edition of *Looking Backward*.

22. For "The Religion of Solidarity" see Joseph Shiffmann, ed., *Edward Bellamy: Selected Writings on Religion and Society* (New York: Liberal Arts Press, 1955).

23. "How I Came to Write 'Looking Backward.' "

24. For an interesting discussion of the "Aesthetics of Utopia," including some remarks on Bellamy and "Berrian," see Elliott, pp. 102-128.

25. Cited by Thomas, p. 63.

26. Le Corbusier, *La ville radieuse* (Boulogne: Éditions de l'architecture d'aujourd'hui, 1935) and *The Radiant City* (New York: Orion Press, 1967). See also Robert Fishman, *Urban Utopias in the Twentieth Century* (New York: Basic Books, 1977).

27. Robert Elliott describes utopia's fall from grace in his chapter, "The Fear of Utopia," pp. 84-101. See also Chad Walsh, *From Utopia to Nightmare* (New York: Harper & Row, 1962), pp. 70-135.

28. At the rate of about a book a year in the decade following the publication of Bellamy's novel, authors in the United States and abroad, including Richard Michaelis (*Looking Forward*) and Philip Wasserburg (*Etwas Später*), attempted to portray the horrors of utopian socialism.

29. Alex M. Shane, *The Life and Works of Eugenij Zamjatin* (Berkeley: University of California Press, 1968). For a consideration of Zamiatin in the context of these other writers, see Edward James Brown, *Brave New World, 1984, We: An Essay on Anti-Utopia* (Ann Arbor: University of Michigan Press, 1976).

30. In *1984 Revisited* (New York: Harper & Row, 1983) Irving Howe notes that the anti-utopian writer is most successful in his depiction of horror "precisely at the moment when the balance teeters between minimal credence and plummeting disbelief. For

it is at such a moment we ask ourselves: Can things really go this far? And it is then that our deepest anxieties are aroused" (p. 8).

31. Orwell's appendix to *1984*, "The Principles of Newspeak," is perhaps the most chilling part of the novel, certainly the most brilliant.

32. John Rodden, "Orwell & Catholicism: the religious fellow traveler," *Commentary* (7 September 1984): 466-70.

33. See Judith D. Shklar, *After Utopia: The Decline of a Political Faith* (Princeton, NJ: Princeton University Press, 1957).

34. Robert Elliott discusses both *Walden Two* and *Island* in his chapter "Anti-Anti-Utopia," pp. 129-153.

35. Glenn Negley and J. Max Patrick, editors of *The Quest for Utopia* (New York: Harry Schuman, 1952), refer to Skinner's work as "a nadir of ignominy in which [man] is placed on a par with pigeons" (p. 590).

36. B. F. Skinner, *Beyond Freedom and Dignity* (New York: Bantam Books, 1972): "What is being abolished is the autonomous man—the inner man, the homunculus, the possessing demon, the man defended by the literatures of freedom and dignity. . . . To man *qua* man we readily say good riddance. Only by dispossessing him can we turn to the real causes of human behavior" (p. 191). It is uncanny to reflect on the degree to which Skinner's vocabulary is echoed in Zamiatin and Orwell.

37. Walker Percy, *The Message in the Bottle* (New York: Farrar, Straus & Giroux, 1975), p. 112. In the first essay, "The Delta Factor," Percy takes on the behaviorists. Compare Skinner in *Science and Human Behavior* (New York: Macmillan, 1953) for a diagnosis that is similar yet based on utterly different assumptions as to cause: "Man's power appears to have increased out of all proportion to his wisdom. He has never been in a better position to build a healthy, happy and productive world; yet things have perhaps never seemed so black" (p. 5).

Cowley Publications is a work of the Society of St. John the
Evangelist, a religious community for men in the Episcopal
Church. The books we publish are a significant part of our
ministry, together with the work of preaching, spiritual direction,
and hospitality. Our aim is to provide books that will enrich their
readers' religious experience and challenge it with fresh approaches
to religious concerns.

BT738 .H33 1985   c.1
Hawkins, Peter S. cn   100105 000
Getting nowhere : Christian ho

3 9310 00077770 4
GOSHEN COLLEGE-GOOD LIBRARY